the BIG PLANT-BASED DIET COOKBOOK

A Stunning Collection Vibrant, Kitchen-Tested Recipes for Healthy Living and Eating Well Every Day

Eva Evans

TEXT COPYRIGHT © EVA EVANS

All rights reserved. No part of this guide may be reproduced in any form without permission in writing from the publisher except in the case of brief quotations embodied in critical articles or reviews.

LEGAL & DISCLAIMER

The information contained in this book and its contents is not designed to replace or take the place of any form of medical or professional advice; and is not meant to replace the need for independent medical, financial, legal, or other professional advice or services, as may be required. The content and information in this book has been provided for educational and entertainment purposes only.

The content and information contained in this book has been compiled from sources deemed reliable, and it is accurate to the best of the Author's knowledge, information, and belief. However, the Author cannot guarantee its accuracy and validity and cannot be held liable for any errors and/or omissions. Further, changes are periodically made to this book as and when needed. Where appropriate and/or necessary, you must consult a professional (including but not limited to your doctor, attorney, financial advisor, or such other professional advisor) before using any of the suggested remedies, techniques, or information in this book.

Upon using the contents and information contained in this book, you agree to hold harmless the Author from and against any damages, costs, and expenses, including any legal fees potentially resulting from the application of any of the information provided by this book. This disclaimer applies to any loss, damages or injury caused by the use and application, whether directly or indirectly, of any advice or information presented, whether for breach of contract, tort, negligence, personal injury, criminal intent, or under any other cause of action.

You agree to accept all risks of using the information presented inside this book. You agree that by continuing to read this book, where appropriate and/or necessary, you shall consult a professional (including but not limited to your doctor, attorney, or financial advisor or such other advisor as needed) before using any of the suggested remedies, techniques, or information in this book.

TABLE OF CONTENTS

DESCRIPTION	6
INTRODUCTION	8
WHAT IS A PLANT-BASED DIET?	10
BENEFITS OF PLANT-BASED DIET	12
FOODS TO EAT AND AVOID	18
BREAKFAST RECIPES	20
Strawberries and Chia Breakfast	22
Chickpea Scramble Bowl	24
Spinach Smoothie	26
Vegan Mango Almond Milkshake	29
Instant Pot Apple Cranberry Oats	30
Scrambled Tofu on Toast	32
Banana Strawberry Oats	34
Super Green Super Apple Cucumber Smoothie	37
Coconut Buckwheat Porridge	38
Raspberry Overnight Oats	40
Tropical Oats With Mango	43
Perfect Polenta with a Dose of Cranberries & Pears	44
WBreakfast Shake	46
Tasty Oatmeal Muffins	48
Strawberry Chamomile Smoothies	51
Ginger Detox Smoothie	52
Pink Smoothie	54
Maca Frap	57
Berry Chia Oats	58
Peanut Butter Vanilla Green Shake	61
Chocolate Oat Smoothie	63
Berry Avocado Smoothie	64
Chickpea Cookie Dough	66
Peach Crumble Shake	68
Nutty Banana Oats	70
Wild Ginger Green Smoothie	73
Vegan Mango Almond Milkshake	74
Peach & Chia Seed Breakfast Parfait	76
Carrot Apple Smoothie	79
Spiced Strawberry Smoothie	80
MAIN DISHES	82
Grilled Zucchini with Tomato Salsa	84
Black Bean Stuffed Sweet Potatoes	86
Ruby Red Root Beet Burger	88
Creamy Squash Pizza	90
Cauliflower with Anchovies Salad	92
Avocado and Cauliflower Hummus	94
Cucumber Edamame Salad	96
Corn Chowder	98
Coconut Veggie Wraps	100
Tasty Cucumber Avocado Sandwich	102
Rice and Bean Burritos	104
Lemon Artichokes	106
Sweet Potato Quesadillas	108
Barbecued Greens & Grits	110
Sweet Potato Sushi	112
Coconut Tofu Curry	114
Chickpea And Spinach Cutlets	116

Brussels Sprout Salad	119
Flavorful Refried Beans	120
Smoky Red Beans and Rice	122
Sizzling Vegetarian Fajitas	125
Rich Red Lentil Curry	127
Mashed Cauliflower	128
Savory Spanish Rice	130
Exquisite Banana, Apple, and Coconut Curry	132
Raw Zoodles with Avocado 'N Nuts	134
Delightful Coconut Vegetarian Curry	136
Creamy Sweet Potato & Coconut Curry	138
Bolognese Pasta	140
Comforting Chickpea Tagine	142
Cauliflower Bolognese with Zucchini Noodles	144
Black Bean and Quinoa Salad	147
Eggplant Parmesan	148
Coconut Chickpea Curry	150
Green Bean Warm Salad	152
Sun-Dried Tomato Pesto Pasta	155
Cauliflower Steak with Sweet-pea Puree	156
Spinach and Mashed Tofu Salad	158
Sweet Potato and White Bean Skillet	160
Spiced Okra	162
Balsamic-Glazed Roasted Cauliflower	165
Asian Brussels Sprouts	166
Carrot Cashew Pate	168
Linguine with Wild Mushrooms	171
Tomato with Tofu	172
Edamame and Noodle Salad	174
Pilaf with Garbanzos and Dried Apricots	176
Veggie Kabobs	178
Spaghetti with Chickpeas Meatballs	180
Apple Lentil Salad	182
Beet Salad	184
Quinoa Edamame Salad	186
Cabbage with Carrot	188
Black Bean Wrap with Hummus	190
DESSERTS AND SNACKS	192
Baked Carrot Chips	194
Brownie Energy Bites	196
Pickled Cucumber Salad	199
Chili Asparagus	200
Sweet Cinnamon Chips	202
Cauliflower Popcorn	205
Garlicky Bell Peppers	206
Rainbow Fruit Salad	208
Chili Parsnip	210
Dark Chocolate Bars	213
Almond Millet Chews	214
Chocolate Peanut Butter Energy Bites	217
Raspberry Compote	218
Simple Banana Cookies	221
Peach Crisp	222
Cookie Dough Bites	224
CONCLUSION	227

DESCRIPTION

If you have never been on a plant-based eating plan, then you must surely have several questions. In general, newcomers to a plant-based eating plan are concerned about getting the right amount of nutrition, which, of course, is always a valid concern. This is exactly why I have chosen to write this book. The intention of this project is to answer all of your questions while helping you implement a new, healthy eating plan.

Herein lies an important consideration: if you're looking to begin on a plant-based eating journey, then you need to have the right guidelines. Otherwise, you may find that you are depriving yourself of the essential nutrients that are necessary for a healthy body. That is why we need to explore the best ways in which you can make sure that you have the right balance of nutrition with every meal.

Plant-based diets are largely successful because they eliminate the use of processed foods that can adversely affect our bodies while fueling it with natural and healthy foods.

The major topics you will encounter in this book include:
- An introduction to the plant-based diet
- The benefits of switching to the diet
- What you can eat and what to avoid
- Breakfast recipes
- Main dishes
- Snacks and desserts
- And much more!!

This cookbook allows you to take care of yourself in a simple, affordable, and nourishing way, without sacrificing flavor or taste. Start cooking with these plant-based recipes today, as making this change could save your life!

INTRODUCTION

It's just you, empowered in your wealth of wellness, progressing along in your everyday life. What an excellent, plant-based ride!

As always, please consult with your regular physician about going on the plant-based eating plan, and don't forget to double-check in case there are any recommendations that your physician might make. This is important, especially considering if you have any food allergies to note or if you have a health condition that may require supervision.

Beyond that, you will find that the plant-based eating plan is a great way to help you manage any chronic medical conditions you may have, boost your energy, and improve your overall quality of life. By getting rid of some of the most toxic foods that we usually consume, you will find that your body will be so much better off for it.

In the end, you have nothing to lose but a few pounds, and everything to gain. Those that have made the switch to the plant-based eating plan have seen significant results in a matter of a few short weeks. These results range from improved energy levels and sleep, to losing weight and relief for existing medical conditions.

WHAT IS A PLANT-BASED DIET?

This diet means consuming plant-derived food products such as greens, grains, fruits, and nuts. The individual can choose the level of restrictions on meat and other products. Being a vegan is not the only way to become someone who eats a plant-based diet. There are several types:

Flexitarian- Those that follow this diet do not entirely cut off any kind of food. They can eat dairy, meat, and seafood. It's according to the person's needs.

Pescatarian -As the name suggests, in this diet, along with plants, you can eat seafood and eggs without hesitation.

Vegetarian- Those that eat eggs and other dairy products with plant-based foods. They cannot eat fish or any meat.

Vegan- They are strict plant-based food eaters who eat nothing in their diet but plant-derived foods.

Plants can provide high nutrients filled with protein and fat and lots of fiber, but it lacks a few minerals and vitamins. You can compensate for them by adding store-bought supplements to the diet.

BENEFITS OF PLANT-BASED DIET

A plant-based diet is an all healthy and natural diet that comes directly from the plants and based on wholeness. The core feature of the diet is no processing involved or mixing either for that matter.

There are many benefits to obtain while following this diet, like the overall increase in wellness and spending less time feeling unwell. Some of them are listed below:

- It is an excellent way to lose weight. Most people commonly get attracted to the plant-based diet because they want to lose weight. The diet contains all-natural food items obtained from the plants, and are available in their raw form. The diet does not involve any processed food options, so everything a person eats takes time to digest. The slow and steady digestion helps metabolism to work efficiently and reduce the body fats in its result. On the other hand, the calorie intake with a proper measurement helps to make things better in losing weight.
- Plant-based foods are full of carbs and fiber, which fills up the stomach quickly, making you feel less hungry. You will consume less of the foods that will be no good for you like sodas or candies. Cravings will not hit you as hard as if you were hungry.
- There is a higher quantity of water in plant-based food, which increases body metabolism and reduces appetite. Water has many benefits; being hydrated makes you have better hair, skin, and makes you look fresh.
- Reduce heart problems. The primary reason for health-related issues is the fat in blood, veins, and body as well. When our blood becomes thick, or there is too much fat in the blood vessels, it is hard for the heart to pump it through them. It can directly lead to more chances of stroke, heart attack, and many other problems. Plant-based diet simply removes the fat factor from your body, blood, and vessels as well. It helps you to burn out all the fat naturally and stop its further production or storage in the body. Eventually, the heart can work adequately to make things better with improved performance.

- Balanced level of cholesterol and hypertension. The plant-based diet works on your progressive health that reduces fats in the body, which leads to lower levels of cholesterol and hypertension. The food options in the diet not only make your body improve its condition, they give you psychological satisfaction as well. When you are satisfied with what you are eating, you will not feel any stress or pressure. This feeling of calmness and satisfaction helps you to get better in life and improve your health conditions.
- Avoid cognitive decline. Eating clean always help your brain to function correctly. What we eat affects not only our body and other organ but also the brain. Eating junk food, processed meals, or meat can affect your cognition severely.
- Reduce the risk of cancer. The best prevention of cancer is the balanced diet and healthy lifestyle, and plant-based diet offers you both. You will not only eat clean but will have clean thoughts and ideas too. All you need is to make sure that you are not suffering from any severe infection in the body. As a whole, the diet helps you to detox your body and reduce all the proliferating chances of cancer in the body.
- No chances of diabetes. Multiple things can trigger diabetes in the body. Other than the genetic reasons for diebetes, our food is the next big cause. It is purely a food-based disease that triggers alongside the increase in blood sugar level and reduced efficient functions of the liver. The consumption of more fast food, no meal pattern, a lack of physical exercise can lead a person to face the critical conditions of diabetes. In case of plant-based diet, it helps to reduce the risk by giving stomach time to digest the meal and helps liver to work properly.
- Better organ health. A plant-based diet is good for not only a specific organ like liver, heart, or kidneys, but it helps your overall body to have smoother operation. It gives proper attention to all the organs and makes it possible for a person to have the best of health in any manner. Other than organs, the diet helps to increase muscular strength, make bones stronger, and hair longer. It is all about how you are managing the diet, and you will be able to get the best results within a few days of starting with it.

- Boost health. The plant-based diet is a healthy diet plan that helps to lift up the health status of a person. The reason for the diet is not only to promote the organic, low fat, and nutrient diet but also to give people optimal health. After knowing the dangers of meat diet and processed food, this is the only way out. The plants are the ultimate sources for nutrition as they are the producers. It is always good to use these nutrients in our daily food intake so we will be able to live a healthy life. The diet allows you to pay attention to each aspect of your health, and it makes your health better with overall improvement.
- Environment-Friendly. By following this diet, you will not only help yourself in becoming better but also push the environment to progress in the right direction. A lot of pollutants come from barns and livestock farms. Raising livestock puts a tremendous strain on the health of our planet, and by consuming less of it, you are leaving less of a carbon footprint. By undertaking a plant-based diet, you are also promoting a healthier lifestyle for others. The plant-based diet is environmentally friendly. When masses are following the plant-based diet, that means there will be more plants and no more packing food. No processed or packaged food means there won't be any disposal or trash out there. On the other hand, more plants will provide more oxygen for people and give them nutrients through food. It is an excellent package for the ultimate healthy and happy society.

- Improving nature interaction. With the help of a plant-based diet, people are getting closer to nature. It helps let people know about all the benefits and advantages of nature, along with natural fruits and plants. Almost everyone wants to have a plant in the house, so it can help him or her to have a fresh supply of essential herbs at least. It is one of the fantastic benefits of the plant-based diet that it is making people friends with plants and nature again.
- It doesn't require any sort of investment, and a person can begin it as soon as they decide to. Plant-based products are everywhere and, even in a normal diet, take a big portion of it. Some dieting programs and fads take a lot of money from people giving only temporary results, but this diet has shown to reduce the most amount of weight.

For some people starting this diet can be hard, but if you want to reach your weight loss goals or generally become more fit, than this diet is suited for you.

FOODS TO EAT AND AVOID

You Can Eat:

- All vegetables, including greens like spinach, kale, chards, collards, asparagus, broccoli, cauliflower, bell peppers, tomatoes, onion, etc
- All fruits, including berries, avocados, apples, bananas, watermelons, grapes, oranges, etc
- Plant-based alternates to meat like tofu and tempeh
- Plant-based milk and dairy products including coconut milk, almond milk, peanut butter, almond butter, cashew yogurt, etc
- All whole-grains, including brown rice, amaranth, quinoa, barley, all beans, whole wheat pasta, whole-grain bread, etc
- All nuts, including cashews, almonds, walnuts, macadamia nuts, etc
- All seeds like chia seeds, flaxseed, hempseeds, etc
- Lentils
- Millets
- Flax eggs
- Honey, maple syrup, coconut sugar, stevia, Splenda, erythritol, etc
- Unsweetened coffee and tea

Foods You Should Avoid:

- Meat including beef, pork, and poultry
- Seafood including fish and shrimp
- Processed animal products like hot dogs or sausages
- Dairy items like butter, eggs, whole milk, yogurt, etc
- Sweetened drinks like soda, fruit juices, sweetened tea, or coffee
- Fried food and fast foods
- White bread and white pasta

BREAKFAST RECIPES

21

STRAWBERRIES AND CHIA BREAKFAST

 Cooking Difficulty: 1/10

 Cooking Time: 10 minutes

 Servings: 2

INGREDIENTS

- 2 tbsps. chopped almonds
- 1 tbsp. chia seeds
- 2 tbsps. roasted pepitas
- 1/3 c. oat milk
- 1/3 c. water
- a handful strawberries

STEP 1
In your food processor, mix pepitas with almonds and pulse them well.

STEP 2
In your instant pot, mix chia seeds with water and oat milk and stir.

STEP 3
Add pepitas mix, stir, cover pot and cook on High for 5 minutes.

STEP 4
Add strawberries, toss a bit, divide into 2 bowls and serve for breakfast.

NUTRITIONAL INFORMATION
150 Calories, 4g Carbs, 2g Protein, 1g Fat

CHICKPEA SCRAMBLE BOWL

 Cooking Difficulty: 2/10

 Cooking Time: 15 minutes

 Servings: 2

INGREDIENTS

- ¼ diced onion
- 15 oz. chickpeas
- 2 garlic cloves, minced
- ½ tsp. turmeric
- ½ tsp. black pepper
- ½ tsp. extra virgin olive oil
- ½ tsp. salt

STEP 1
Begin by placing the chickpeas in a large bowl along with a bit of water. Soak for few minutes and then mash the chickpeas lightly with a fork while leaving some of them in the whole form.

STEP 2
Next, spoon in the turmeric, pepper, and salt to the bowl. Mix well.

STEP 3
Then, heat oil in a medium-sized skillet over medium-high heat.

STEP 4
Once the oil becomes hot, stir in the onions. Sauté the onions for 3 to 4 minutes or until softened.

STEP 5
Then, add the garlic and cook for further 1 minute or until aromatic.

STEP 6
After that, stir in the mashed chickpeas. Cook for another 4 minutes or until thickened.

STEP 7
Serve along with micro greens. Place the greens at the bottom, followed by the scramble, and top it with cilantro or parsley. Serve alongside avocado slices.

NUTRITIONAL INFORMATION
Calories: 801, Proteins: 41.5g, Carbs: 131.6g, Fat: 14.7g

SPINACH SMOOTHIE

 Cooking Difficulty: 1/10	 Cooking Time: 2 minutes	 Servings: 1

INGREDIENTS

- 3c. spinach
- 1 c. chopped kale leaves
- 2 c. water
- mint leaves
- ice cubes
- 1 tsp. spirulina

STEP 1
Except for the mint leaves, add everything in a blender and blend until smooth.

STEP 2
Garnish with mint leaves and serve.

NUTRITIONAL INFORMATION
Calories: 79, Fat: 1g, Carbs: 12.9g, Protein: 9g

VEGAN MANGO ALMOND MILKSHAKE

 Cooking Difficulty: 1/10

 Cooking Time: 2 minutes

 Servings: 1

INGREDIENTS

- 1 ripe mango, pulp
- ¾ c. unsweetened almond milk
- ½ c. ice

STEP 1
Grab your blender, add the ingredients and whizz until smooth.

STEP 2
Serve and enjoy.

NUTRITIONAL INFORMATION
Calories 232, Fat 3.9g, Carbs 51.8g, Protein 3.5g

INSTANT POT APPLE CRANBERRY OATS

 Cooking Difficulty: 2/10

 Cooking Time: 12 minutes

 Servings: 6

INGREDIENTS

- 2 c. oats
- 2 tbsps. butter
- 2 c. whole milk
- 1 c. almond milk
- 3 c. water
- 3 apples, peeled and diced
- 1½ c. cranberries
- ¼ tsp. salt
- ½ tsp. cinnamon
- 1 tbsp. lemon juice
- 2 tsp. vanilla extract
- ¼ c. maple syrup

STEP 1
In a bowl, soak the maple syrup with vanilla extract for about an hour.

STEP 2
In your IP, set in your butter to SAUTÉ. Add the oats and fry for about a minute.

STEP 3
Add the water, whole milk, followed by almond milk, and give it a stir. Add the maple syrup mixture and stir again.

STEP 4
Sprinkle with the cinnamon powder and salt and close the lid.

STEP 5
Choose MANUAL, and cook at high pressure for 10 minutes.

STEP 6
When the cooking is complete, do a natural pressure release.

STEP 7
Open the lid, and add the lemon juice and gently mix.

STEP 8
Garnish with diced apples and cranberries and serve.

NUTRITIONAL INFORMATION
Calories: 383; Fat: 18.1g; Carbs: 43.3g; Protein: 7.5g

SCRAMBLED TOFU ON TOAST

INGREDIENTS

- 2 tbsps. olive oil
- ½ c. onion, minced
- 1 tbsp. minced garlic
- ¼ c. diced tomatoes
- ¼ c. diced red bell pepper
- ¼ tsp. turmeric powder
- ½ c. vegetable stock
- ¼ tsp. salt
- 1/16 tsp. black pepper
- ⅛ c. minced green onions
- 2 tbsps. cashew cheese
- 2 sprigs parsley, for garnish
- 2 toasted, thick-cut bread
- 1 pack extra firm

STEP 1
Press the "saute" button of the Instant Pot. Pour olive oil. Once hot, saute onion, garlic, and tomatoes for 3 minutes or until limp.

STEP 2
Add in red bell pepper, turmeric powder, vegetable stock, salt, and black pepper.

STEP 3
Close the lid. Lock in place and make sure to seal the valve. Press the manual button and cook for 1 minute on high.

STEP 4
When the timer beeps, choose the quick pressure release. This would take 1–2 minutes. Remove the lid.

STEP 5
Add in green onions and cashew cheese. Adjust taste if needed.

STEP 6
To serve, spoon "scrambled eggs" on toasted bread. Garnish with parsley sprigs. Serve.

 Cooking Difficulty: 2/10	 Cooking Time: 12 minutes	 Servings: 2

NUTRITIONAL INFORMATION
Calories: 144.1, Fat: 5.7g, Carbs: 11.8g, Protein: 13.9g

BANANA STRAWBERRY OATS

 Cooking Difficulty: 1/10

 Cooking Time: 15 minutes

 Servings: 1

INGREDIENTS
- 1 tbsp. sliced almonds
- ½ c. oats
- ½ tsp. cinnamon
- 1 c. shredded zucchini
- ½ banana, mashed
- 1 c. water
- ½ c. sliced strawberries
- dash of sea salt
- 1 tbsp. flax meal
- ½ scoop of protein powder

STEP 1
First, combine oats, salt, water, and zucchini in a large saucepan.

STEP 2
Cook the mixture over medium-high heat and cook for 8 to 10 minutes or until the liquid is absorbed.

STEP 3
Now, spoon in all the remaining ingredients to the mixture and give everything a good stir.

STEP 4
Finally, transfer the mixture to a serving bowl and top it with almonds and berries. Serve and enjoy.

NUTRITIONAL INFORMATION
Calories: 386, Proteins: 23.7g, Carbs: 57.5g, Fat: 8.9g

SUPER GREEN SUPER APPLE CUCUMBER SMOOTHIE

 Cooking Difficulty: 1/10

 Cooking Time: 2 minutes

 Servings: 1

INGREDIENTS

- ¼ c. lime juice, freshly squeezed
- 1 cored apple
- 1 c. baby spinach
- 1 cucumber
- 1 tbsp. raw honey
- 1 tbsp. minced ginger
- 1 c. water

STEP 1

Using a blender, set in all your ingredients and blend until very smooth. Enjoy!

NUTRITIONAL INFORMATION

Calories: 229, Fat: 1.1 g, Carbs: 59 g, Protein: 3.9 g

COCONUT BUCKWHEAT PORRIDGE

 Cooking Difficulty: 2/10	 Cooking Time: 12 minutes	 Servings: 6

INGREDIENTS

- 1 c. water
- 2 tsps. vanilla extract
- 1 c. buckwheat grouts
- dash of salt
- ¼ c. chia seeds
- ¼ tsp. cinnamon
- 3 c. unsweetened coconut milk

STEP 1
For making this high-protein oatmeal, you need to mix all the ingredients in a large mixing bowl until combined well.

STEP 2
Then, cover the bowl with plastic cling and place it in the refrigerator overnight.

STEP 3
Next morning, transfer the contents to a deep saucepan over medium heat.

STEP 4
Cook for 10 minutes or until thickened. Tip: Make sure to stir it continuously.

STEP 5
Serve it hot or warm.

NUTRITIONAL INFORMATION
Calories: 387, Proteins: 7g, Carbs: 25.3g, Fat: 31.4g

RASPBERRY OVERNIGHT OATS

 Cooking Difficulty: 2/10	 Cooking Time: 5 minutes	 Servings: 2

INGREDIENTS

- 1 tsp. maple syrup
- ¼ c. white beans
- ¼ c. raspberries
- ½ c. rolled oats
- 10 raw almonds, chopped
- 1 tsp. chia seeds
- 2/3 c. soy milk

STEP 1
To start with, place the beans in a large mason jar and mash it with a fork.

STEP 2
Next, stir in all the remaining ingredients to the Mason jar. Mix well.

STEP 3
Now, keep the jar in the refrigerator overnight.

STEP 4
In the morning, keep the Mason jar out of the refrigerator and mix well.

STEP 5
Serve immediately and enjoy it.

NUTRITIONAL INFORMATION
Calories: 371, Proteins: 16.8g, Carbs: 54.5g, Fat: 11.4g

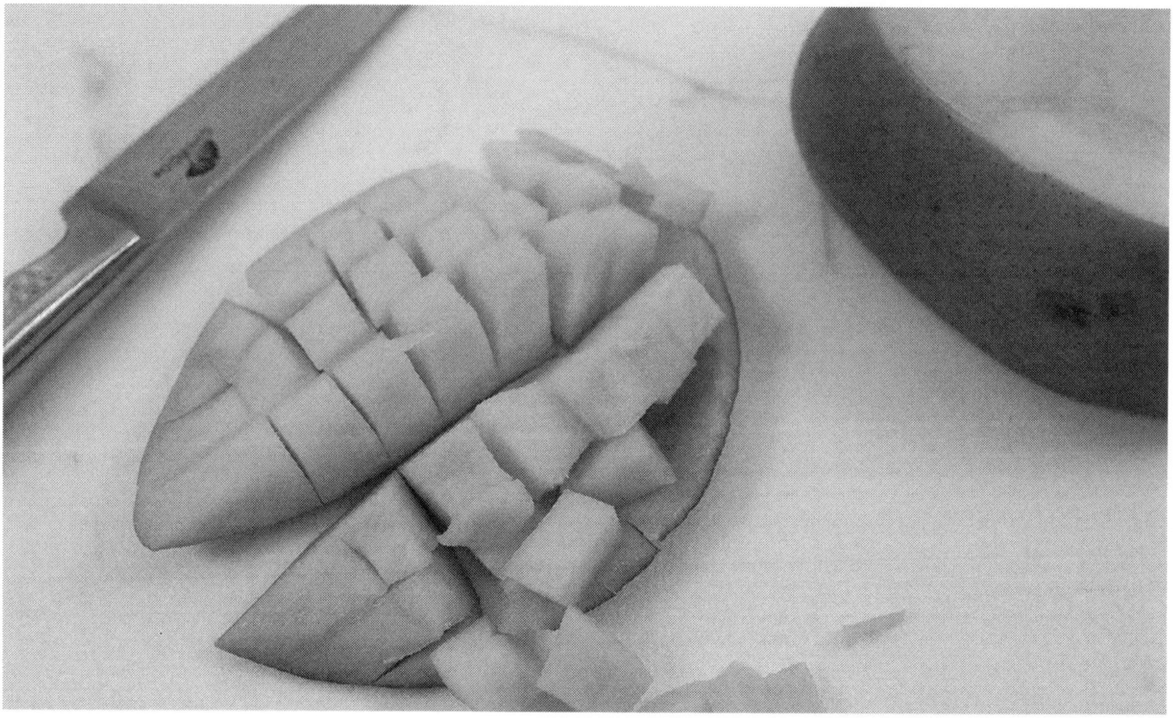

42

TROPICAL OATS WITH MANGO

 Cooking Difficulty: 2/10

 Cooking Time: 25 minutes

 Servings: 2

INGREDIENTS

- 1 tsp. coconut oil
- ¼ c. steel cut oats
- 2 c. water
- 1½ c. mashed bananas
- ½ c. cubed ripe mangoes
- 2 c. oat milk
- ½ c. chopped cashew nuts

STEP 1
Lightly grease crockpot with coconut oil.

STEP 2
Pour oats, water, and bananas into the Instant Pot. Stir mixture well.

STEP 3
Close the lid. Lock in place and make sure to seal the valve. Press the manual button and cook for 12 minutes on high.

STEP 4
When the timer beeps, choose the natural pressure release. This would take 7–10 minutes. Remove the lid.

STEP 5
To serve, divide oats into 2 bowls. Pour milk. Garnish with cashew nuts and mangoes.

NUTRITIONAL INFORMATION
Calories: 136; Fat: 2g; Carbs: 28g; Protein: 2g

PERFECT POLENTA WITH A DOSE OF CRANBERRIES & PEARS

 Cooking Difficulty: 2/10

 Cooking Time: 12 minutes

 Servings: 4

INGREDIENTS

- 2 freshly cored pears, peeled and diced
- 1 batch warm basic polenta
- ¼ c. brown rice syrup
- 1 tsp. cinnamon, ground
- 1 c. fresh cranberries

STEP 1
In a saucepan, add in polenta and warm. Stir in pears, cinnamon powder, and cranberries.

STEP 2
Cook until pears become soft in 10 minutes.

STEP 3
Divide in 4 bowls. Top with some pear compote. Serve.

NUTRITIONAL INFORMATION
Calories: 185, Fat 4.6 g, Protein 5 g, carbs 6.1 g

BREAKFAST SHAKE

 Cooking Difficulty: 1/10

 Cooking Time: 1 minutes

 Servings: 1

INGREDIENTS

- 3 tbsps. raw cacao powder
- 1 c. soy/almond milk
- 2 frozen bananas
- 3 tbsps. natural peanut butter

STEP 1
Set all ingredients in a blender.

STEP 2
Blend well to get a smooth shake.

STEP 3
Enjoy.

NUTRITIONAL INFORMATION
Calories: 330, Fat 15 g, Carbs 41 g, Protein 11 g

TASTY OATMEAL MUFFINS

 Cooking Difficulty: 3/10

 Cooking Time: 30 minutes

 Servings: 2

INGREDIENTS

- ½ c. hot water
- ½ c. raisins
- ¼ c. ground flaxseed
- 2 c. rolled oats
- ¼ tsp. sea salt
- ½ c. walnuts
- ¼ tsp. baking soda
- 1 banana
- 2 tbsps. cinnamon
- ¼ c. maple syrup

STEP 1
Mix water with flaxseed and set aside for about 5 minutes.

STEP 2
Set the flaxsees mixture with the rest of the ingredients in a food processor. Blend well for approximately 30 seconds to get a semi-coarse batter.

STEP 3
Set the batter in cupcake liners and transfer in muffin tins.

STEP 4
Set oven to preheat at 350 degrees F and bake for 20 minutes.

STEP 5
Serve.

NUTRITIONAL INFORMATION
Calories: 133, Fat 2 g, Carbs 27 g, Protein 3 g

STRAWBERRY CHAMOMILE SMOOTHIES

 Cooking Difficulty: 1/10

 Cooking Time: 1 minutes

 Servings: 1

INGREDIENTS
- 1¾ c. chilled brewed chamomile tea
- 2 c. frozen strawberries
- 2 tbsps. lemon juice, freshly squeezed
- ½ c. white mulberries, dried
- 2 tbsps. chia seeds

STEP 1
Using a blender, set in all the ingredients and blend well until very smooth.

STEP 2
Enjoy!

NUTRITIONAL INFORMATION
Calories: 232, Fat: 5.7 g, Carbs: 48.1 g, Protein: 5.2 g

GINGER DETOX SMOOTHIE

 Cooking Difficulty: 1/10

 Cooking Time: 1 minutes

 Servings: 2

INGREDIENTS

- 1 chopped apple
- 2 chopped persian cucumbers
- 1 peeled meyer lemon
- ½ tsp. chlorella
- ½ inch ginger
- 1 ½ oz. collard green
- 1 c. water

STEP 1
Add all the listed ingredients to a blender.

STEP 2
Process well to obtain a smooth and creamy texture.

STEP 3
Serve chilled and enjoy!

NUTRITIONAL INFORMATION
Calories: 114, Fat: 1g, Carbs: 22g, Protein: 5g

PINK SMOOTHIE

 Cooking Difficulty: 1/10

 Cooking Time: 3 minutes

 Servings: 1

INGREDIENTS

- 1 peeled clementine, segmented
- ½ banana, frozen
- 1 peeled beet, chopped
- 1/8 tsp. sea salt
- ½ c. raspberries
- 1 tbsp. chia seeds
- ¼ tsp. unsweetened vanilla extract
- 2 tbsps. almond butter
- 1 c. unsweetened almond milk

STEP 1

Place all the ingredients in the order in a food processor or blender and then pulse for 2 to 3 minutes at high speed until smooth.

STEP 2

Pour the smoothie into a glass and then serve.

NUTRITIONAL INFORMATION

Calories: 278, Fat: 5.6 g, Carbs: 37.2 g, Protein: 6.2 g

MACA FRAP

 Cooking Difficulty: 1/10	 Cooking Time: 3 minutes	 Servings: 4

INGREDIENTS

- ½ frozen banana, sliced
- ¼ c. cashews, soaked
- 2 pitted medjool dates
- 1 tsp. maca powder
- 1/8 tsp. sea salt
- ½ tsp. unsweetened vanilla extract
- ¼ c. unsweetened almond milk
- ¼ c. cold coffee, brewed

STEP 1
Place all the ingredients in the order in a food processor or blender and then pulse for 2 to 3 minutes at high speed until smooth.

STEP 2
Pour the smoothie into a glass and then serve.

NUTRITIONAL INFORMATION
Calories: 450, Fat: 170 g, Carbs: 64 g, Protein: 7 g

BERRY CHIA OATS

 Cooking Difficulty: 2/10	 Cooking Time: 20 minutes	 Servings: 2

NUTRITIONAL INFORMATION
Calories: 114, Fat: 3g, Carbs: 18g, Protein: 4.5g

INGREDIENTS

- ½ c. old fashioned oats
- ½ c. unsweetened almond milk
- ½ c. blueberries
- 1 tsp. chia seeds
- sweetener
- splash of vanilla
- ¼ tsp. salt
- ¼ tsp. ground cinnamon
- 1½ c. water

STEP 1
In a bowl, mix all ingredients. Add the bowl mixture to a pint-size jar and cover with an aluminum foil.

STEP 2
In the pot, slowly pour the water. Take the trivet and arrange inside it; place the jar over it.

STEP 3
Close the lid and lock. Ensure that you have sealed the valve to avoid leakage.

STEP 4
Press "Manual" mode and set a timer for 6 minutes. It will take a few minutes for the pot to build inside pressure and start cooking.

STEP 5
After the timer reads zero, press "Cancel" and naturally release pressure. It takes about 8-10 minutes to release pressure naturally.

STEP 6
Carefully remove the lid and take out the jar. Mix in the oatmeal; serve warm!

PEANUT BUTTER VANILLA GREEN SHAKE

 Cooking Difficulty: 1/10

 Cooking Time: 3 minutes

 Servings: 1

INGREDIENTS
- 1 tsp. flax seeds
- 1 banana, frozen
- 1 c. baby spinach
- 1/8 tsp. sea salt
- ½ tsp. cinnamon, ground
- ¼ tsp. unsweetened vanilla extract
- 2 tbsps. unsweetened peanut butter
- ¼ c. ice
- 1 c. coconut milk, unsweetened

STEP 1
Place all the ingredients in the order in a food processor or blender and then pulse for 2 to 3 minutes at high speed until smooth.

STEP 2
Pour the smoothie into a glass and then serve.

NUTRITIONAL INFORMATION
Calories: 298, Fat: 11 g, Carbs: 32 g, Protein: 24 g

CHOCOLATE OAT SMOOTHIE

 Cooking Difficulty: 1/10

 Cooking Time: 3 minutes

 Servings: 1

INGREDIENTS

- ¼ c. rolled oats
- 1 ½ tbsp. unsweetened cocoa powder
- 1 tsp. flax seeds
- 1 frozen banana
- 1/8 tsp. sea salt
- 1/8 tsp. cinnamon
- ¼ tsp. unsweetened vanilla extract
- 2 tbsps. almond butter
- 1 c. unsweetened coconut milk

STEP 1

Place all the ingredients in the order in a food processor or blender and then pulse for 2 to 3 minutes at high speed until smooth.

STEP 2

Pour the smoothie into a glass and then serve.

NUTRITIONAL INFORMATION

Calories: 262, Fat: 7.3 g, Carbs: 50.4 g, Protein: 8.1 g

BERRY AVOCADO SMOOTHIE

 Cooking Difficulty: 1/10

 Cooking Time: 1 minutes

 Servings: 1

INGREDIENTS
- ¼ avocado
- ½ c. red raspberries
- ½ c. blackberries
- 1 whole banana
- ½ c. water

STEP 1
Using a blender, set in all your ingredients and blend until very smooth.

STEP 2
Enjoy!

NUTRITIONAL INFORMATION
Calories: 275, Fat: 8.2g, Carbs: 54 g, Protein: 6 g

CHICKPEA COOKIE DOUGH

 Cooking Difficulty: 1/10	 Cooking Time: 3 minutes	 Servings: 6

NUTRITIONAL INFORMATION
Calories: 415, Protein: 13.9g, Carbs: 54.4g, Fat: 16.9g

INGREDIENTS

- ½ tsp. sea salt
- 2 c. cooked chickpeas, drained
- ¼ c. maple syrup
- 1/3 c. melted coconut oil
- 3 tbsps. coconut flour
- 2 tsps. vanilla extract

STEP 1

To make this delightful cookie dough, first, blend the chickpeas in a high-speed blender for a minute or until smooth.

STEP 2

Spoon in the oil, sea salt, maple syrup, and vanilla extract. Blend for a further minute or until combined.

STEP 3

Next, stir in the coconut flour and blend again. Scrape the sides.

STEP 4

Now, transfer the mixture to a medium-sized bowl and place in the refrigerator for 2 hours.

STEP 5

Serve on its own or with crackers.

PEACH CRUMBLE SHAKE

 Cooking Difficulty: 1/10

 Cooking Time: 3 minutes

 Servings: 1

INGREDIENTS

- 1 tbsp. chia seeds
- ¼ c. rolled oats
- 2 pitted peaches, sliced
- ¾ tsp. ground cinnamon
- 1 pitted medjool date
- ½ tsp. unsweetened vanilla extract
- 2 tbsps. lemon juice
- ½ c. water
- 1 tbsp. coconut butter
- 1 c. unsweetened coconut milk

STEP 1

Place all the ingredients in the order in a food processor or blender and then pulse for 2 to 3 minutes at high speed until smooth.

STEP 2

Pour the smoothie into a glass and then serve.

NUTRITIONAL INFORMATION

Calories: 275, Fat: 8.2g, Carbs: 54 g, Protein: 6 g

NUTTY BANANA OATS

INGREDIENTS

- 2 sliced bananas
- 3 c. water
- 1 tsp. ground cinnamon
- 1 c. oats, steel cut
- ¼ tsp. ground nutmeg
- maple syrup
- ½ c. chopped nuts (almonds, walnuts, pecans, etc.)

STEP 1
Take Instant Pot and carefully arrange it over a clean, dry kitchen platform. Turn on the appliance.

STEP 2
In the cooking pot area, add the water, oats, cinnamon, ginger, and half of the sliced banana. Stir the ingredients gently.

STEP 3
Close the pot lid and seal the valve to avoid any leakage. Find and press "Manual" cooking setting and set cooking time to 3 minutes.

STEP 4
Allow the recipe ingredients to cook for the set time, and after that, the timer reads "zero."

STEP 5
Press "Cancel" and press "NPR" setting for natural pressure release. It takes 8-10 times for all inside pressure to release.

STEP 6
Open the pot and arrange the cooked recipe in serving plates. Top with leftover banana and nuts, and enjoy the vegan recipe!

 Cooking Difficulty: 2/10	 Cooking Time: 10 minutes	 Servings: 2

NUTRITIONAL INFORMATION
Calories: 296, Fat: 9g, Carbs: 42.5g, Protein: 10g

WILD GINGER GREEN SMOOTHIE

 Cooking Difficulty: 1/10

 Cooking Time: 3 minutes

 Servings: 1

INGREDIENTS

- ½ c. pineapple chunks, frozen
- ½ c. kale, chopped
- ½ banana, frozen
- 1 tbsp. lime juice
- 2 inches peeled ginger, chopped
- ½ c. unsweetened coconut milk
- ½ c. coconut water

STEP 1

Place all the ingredients in the order in a food processor or blender and then pulse for 2 to 3 minutes at high speed until smooth.

STEP 2

Pour the smoothie into a glass and then serve.

NUTRITIONAL INFORMATION

Calories: 331, Fat: 14 g, Carbs: 40 g, Protein: 16 g

VEGAN MANGO ALMOND MILKSHAKE

 Cooking Difficulty: 1/10	 Cooking Time: 1 minutes	 Servings: 1

INGREDIENTS
- 1 ripe mango, pulp
- ¾ c. unsweetened almond milk
- ½ c. ice

STEP 1
Grab your blender, add the ingredients and whizz until smooth.

STEP 2
Serve and enjoy.

NUTRITIONAL INFORMATION
Calories 232, Fat 3.9g, Carbs 51.8g, Protein 3.5g

PEACH & CHIA SEED BREAKFAST PARFAIT

 Cooking Difficulty: 2/10	 Cooking Time: 10 minutes	 Servings: 4

NUTRITIONAL INFORMATION
Calories: 415, Protein: 13.9g, Carbs: 54.4g, Fat: 16.9g

INGREDIENTS

- ½ oz. chia seeds
- 1 tbsp. pure maple syrup
- 1 c. coconut milk
- 1 tsp. ground cinnamon
- 3 diced peaches
- 2/3 c. granola

STEP 1
Find a small bowl and add the chia seeds, maple syrup, and coconut milk.

STEP 2
Stir well, then cover and pop into the fridge for at least one hour.

STEP 3
Find another bowl, add the peaches and sprinkle with the cinnamon. Pop to one side.

STEP 4
When it's time to serve, take two glasses, and pour the chia mixture between the two.

STEP 5
Sprinkle the granola over the top, keeping a tiny amount to one side to use to decorate later.

STEP 6
Top with the peaches and top with the reserved granola and serve.

CARROT APPLE SMOOTHIE

 Cooking Difficulty: 1/10

 Cooking Time: 1 minutes

 Servings: 1

INGREDIENTS
- 2 c. baby spinach
- 1 medium apple, cored
- 1 tbsp. ginger, freshly grated
- 2 chopped carrots
- 1 c. filtered water

STEP 1
Using a blender, set in all your ingredients until creamy and smooth. Serve right away!

NUTRITIONAL INFORMATION
Calories: 157, Fat: 0.6 g, Carbs: 36 g, Protein: 4 g

SPICED STRAWBERRY SMOOTHIE

 Cooking Difficulty: 1/10
 Cooking Time: 3 minutes
 Servings: 1

INGREDIENTS

- 1 tbsp. soaked goji berries
- 1 c. strawberries
- 1/8 tsp. sea salt
- 1 frozen banana
- 1 pitted medjool date
- 1 scoop vanilla-flavored whey protein
- 2 tbsps. lemon juice
- ¼ tsp. ground ginger
- ½ tsp. ground cinnamon
- 1 tbsp. almond butter
- 1 c. unsweetened almond milk

STEP 1
Place all the ingredients in the order in a food processor or blender and then pulse for 2 to 3 minutes at high speed until smooth.

STEP 2
Pour the smoothie into a glass and then serve.

NUTRITIONAL INFORMATION
Calories: 182, Fat: 1.3 g, Carbs: 34 g, Protein: 6.4 g

MAIN DISHES

GRILLED ZUCCHINI WITH TOMATO SALSA

 Cooking Difficulty: 3/10	 Cooking Time: 10 minutes	 Servings: 4

INGREDIENTS

- 4 zucchinis, sliced
- 1 tbsp. olive oil
- salt and pepper
- 1 c. tomatoes, chopped
- 1 tbsp. mint, chopped
- 1 tsp. red wine vinegar

STEP 1
Preheat your grill.

STEP 2
Coat the zucchini with oil and season with salt and pepper.

STEP 3
Grill for 4 minutes per side.

STEP 4
Mix the remaining ingredients in a bowl.

STEP 5
Top the grilled zucchini with the minty salsa.

NUTRITIONAL INFORMATION
Calories 71, fat 5 g, carbs 6 g, Protein 2 g

85

BLACK BEAN STUFFED SWEET POTATOES

 Cooking Difficulty: 4/10	 Cooking Time: 80 minutes	 Servings: 4

NUTRITIONAL INFORMATION
Calories: 387, Fat: 16.1 g, Carbs: 53 g, Protein: 10.4 g

INGREDIENTS

- 4 sweet potatoes
- 15 oz. cooked black beans
- ½ tsp. ground black pepper
- ½ red onion, peeled, diced
- ½ tsp. sea salt
- ¼ tsp. onion powder
- ¼ tsp. garlic powder
- ¼ tsp. red chili powder
- ¼ tsp. cumin
- 1 tsp. lime juice
- 1 ½ tbsps. olive oil
- ½ c. cashew cream sauce

STEP 1
Spread sweet potatoes on a baking tray greased with oil and bake for 65 minutes at 350 degrees f until tender.

STEP 2
Meanwhile, prepare the sauce, and for this, whisk together the cream sauce, black pepper, and lime juice until combined, set aside until required.

STEP 3
When 10 minutes of the baking time of potatoes are left, heat a skillet pan with oil. Add in onion to cook until golden for 5 minutes.

STEP 4
Then stir in spice, cook for another 3 minutes, stir in bean until combined and cook for 5 minutes until hot.

STEP 5
Let roasted sweet potatoes cool for 10 minutes, then cut them open, mash the flesh and top with bean mixture, cilantro and avocado, and then drizzle with cream sauce.

STEP 6
Serve straight away.

RUBY RED ROOT BEET BURGER

 Cooking Difficulty: 4/10	 Cooking Time: 32 minutes	 Servings: 6

INGREDIENTS

- 1 c. dry chickpeas
- ½ c. dry quinoa
- 2 beets
- 2 tbsps. olive oil
- 2 tbsps. garlic powder
- 1 tbsp. balsamic vinegar
- ¼ tsp. Salt
- 2 tsps. onion powder
- 1 tsp. freshly chopped parsley
- ¼ tsp. pepper
- 2 c. fresh spinach washed and dried
- 6 buns or wraps of your choice

STEP 1
Preheat the oven to 400°F.

STEP 2
Peel and dice the beets into ¼-inch or smaller cubes, put them in a bowl, and coat the cubes with 1 tablespoon of olive oil and the onion powder.

STEP 3
Spread the beet cubes out across a baking pan and put the pan in the oven.

STEP 4
Roast the beets until they have softened, approximately 10-15 minutes. Take them out and set aside so the beets can cool down.

STEP 5
After the beets have cooled down, transfer them into a food processor and add the cooked chickpeas and quinoa, vinegar, garlic, parsley, and a pinch of pepper and salt.

STEP 6
Pulse the ingredients until everything is crumbly, around 30 seconds.

STEP 7
Use your palms to form the mixture into 6 equal-sized patties and place them in a small pan.

STEP 8
Put them in a freezer, up to 1 hour, until the patties feel firm to the touch.

STEP 9
Heat up the remaining 1 tablespoon of olive oil in a skillet over medium-high heat and add the patties.

STEP 10
Cook them until they're browned on each side, about 4-6 minutes per side.

STEP 11
Store or serve the burgers with a handful of spinach, and if desired, on the bottom of the optional bun.

STEP 12
Top the burger with your sauce of choice.

NUTRITIONAL INFORMATION
Calories 353, Fat 9.2g, Carbs 57.8g, Protein 13.9g

CREAMY SQUASH PIZZA

STEP 1
Preheat the oven to 350°F.

STEP 2
Prepare the French green lentils according to the method.

STEP 3
Add all the sauce ingredients to a food processor or blender, and blend on low until everything has mixed and the sauce looks creamy. Place in a bowl and set aside.

STEP 4
Clean the food processor or blender; then add all the ingredients for the crust and pulse on high speed until a dough-like batter has formed.

STEP 5
Heat a large deep-dish pan over medium-low heat and lightly grease it with 1 tablespoon of olive oil.

STEP 6
Press the crust dough into the skillet until it resembles a round pizza crust and cook until the crust is golden brown—about 5-6 minutes on each side.

STEP 7
Put the crust on a baking tray covered with parchment paper.

STEP 8
Coat the topside of the crust with the sauce using a spoon, and evenly distribute the toppings across the pizza.

STEP 9
Bake the pizza in the oven until the vegetables are tender and browned, for about 15 minutes.

STEP 10
Slice into 4 equal pieces and serve, or store.

NUTRITIONAL INFORMATION
Calories 258, Fat 9.2g, Carbs 38.3g, Protein 9g

INGREDIENTS

- 3 c. fresh butternut squash, cubed
- 2 tbsps. minced garlic
- 1 tbsp. olive oil
- 1 tsp. red pepper flakes
- 1 tsp. cumin
- 1 tsp. paprika
- 1 tsp. oregano

Crust:
- 2 c. dry french green lentils
- 2 c. water
- 2 tbsps. minced garlic
- 1 tbsp. italian seasoning
- 1 tsp. onion powder

Toppings:
- 1 tbsp. olive oil
- 1 pitted green bell pepper, diced
- 1 c. chopped broccoli
- 1 diced purple onion

 Cooking Difficulty: 5/10

 Cooking Time: 30 minutes

 Servings: 4

CAULIFLOWER WITH ANCHOVIES SALAD

 Cooking Difficulty: 2/10

 Cooking Time: 7 minutes

 Servings: 2

INGREDIENTS

- 1 chopped cauliflower head
- ½ c. black olives
- ¾ c. water
- 1 garlic clove
- 1 tbsps. capers
- ¼ c. extra virgin olive oil
- ½ tsp. salt
- 1 tbsp. minced parsley

STEP 1
Pour water into the Instant Pot Pressure Cooker. Place florets into the steamer basket and place on the trivet.

STEP 2
Position the lid and lock in place. Place the Instant Pot Pressure Cooker to high heat and bring to high pressure. Press the Steam button and adjust heat to stabilize the pressure and cook for 2 minutes.

STEP 3
When the timer beeps, choose the quick pressure release. This would take 1–2 minutes. Remove the lid. Turn off the pressure cooker. Carefully remove the lid.

STEP 4
Open the pressure cooker. Rinse the cauliflower with cold water to stop the cooking process. Drain well and put in a serving bowl.

STEP 5
For the vinaigrette, in a food processor, put the oil, capers, garlic, and salt. Blend until smooth. Pour the vinaigrette into the cauliflower and toss.

STEP 6
Garnish with parsley and black olives. Serve.

NUTRITIONAL INFORMATION
Calories: 102, Fat: 10g, Carbs: 3g, Protein: 0g

AVOCADO AND CAULIFLOWER HUMMUS

 Cooking Difficulty: 2/10
 Cooking Time: 32 minutes
 Servings: 2

INGREDIENTS

- 1 cauliflower, stemmed and chopped
- 1 pitted hass avocado, peeled, and chopped
- ¼ c. extra virgin olive oil
- 2 garlic cloves
- ½ tbsp. lemon juice
- ½ tsp. onion powder
- sea salt and ground black pepper
- 2 carrots
- ¼ c. freshly chopped cilantro

STEP 1
Set your oven to 450°F and line a baking tray with aluminum foil.

STEP 2
Put the chopped cauliflower on the baking tray and drizzle with 2 tablespoons of olive oil.

STEP 3
Roast the chopped cauliflower in the oven for 20-25 minutes, until lightly brown.

STEP 4
Remove the tray from the oven and allow the cauliflower to cool down.

STEP 5
Add all the ingredients—except the carrots and optional fresh cilantro—to a food processor or blender, and blend the ingredients into a smooth hummus.

STEP 6
Transfer the hummus to a medium-sized bowl, cover, and put it in the fridge for at least 30 minutes.

STEP 7
Take the hummus out of the fridge and, if desired, top it with the optional chopped cilantro and more salt and pepper to taste; serve with the carrot fries, and enjoy!

NUTRITIONAL INFORMATION
Calories 416, Carbs 8.4 g, Fats 40.3 g, Protein 3.3 g

CUCUMBER EDAMAME SALAD

STEP 1
Bring a medium-sized pot filled halfway with water to a boil over medium-high heat.

STEP 2
Add the sugar snaps peas and cook them for about 2 minutes.

STEP 3
Take the pot off the heat, drain the excess water, transfer the sugar snaps peas to a medium-sized bowl and set aside for now.

STEP 4
Fill the pot with water again, add the teaspoon of salt and bring to a boil over medium-high heat.

STEP 5
Add in edamame and let them cook for about 6 minutes.

STEP 6
Take the pot off the heat, drain the excess water, transfer the soybeans to the bowl with sugar snaps peas, and let them cool down for about 5 minutes.

STEP 7
Using a bowl, mix all ingredients, except sesame seeds and nori crumbs.

STEP 8
Stir well to coat.

STEP 9
Top with sesame seeds and nori crumbs.

STEP 10
Refrigerate for 30 minutes. Serve.

 Cooking Difficulty: 2/10	 Cooking Time: 15 minutes	 Servings: 2

INGREDIENTS

- 3 tbsps. avocado oil
- 1 c. cucumber, sliced
- ½ c. fresh sugar snap peas, sliced
- ½ c. fresh edamame
- ¼ c. radish, sliced
- 1 pitted hass avocado, peeled, sliced
- 1 crumbled nori sheet
- 2 tsps. roasted sesame seeds
- 1 tsp. salt

NUTRITIONAL INFORMATION

Calories 409, Carbs 7.1 g, Fats 38.25 g, Protein 7.6 g

CORN CHOWDER

 Cooking Difficulty: 3/10	 Cooking Time: 10 minutes	 Servings: 6

INGREDIENTS

- 3 c. frozen corn
- 2 c. vegetable broth
- 3 chopped potatoes
- 1 chopped onion
- salt
- pepper
- 2 tbsps. vegan butter
- 2 c. coconut milk

STEP 1
Add the first 5 ingredients to the Instant Pot. Stir everything together.

STEP 2
Close the lid, choose MANUAL, and cook at high pressure for 7 minutes.

STEP 3
When the cooking is complete, press CANCEL and do a quick pressure release.

STEP 4
Open the lid, blend the mixture with a hand blender, until smooth.

STEP 5
Set the pot to SAUTÉ. Add the butter and milk, stir to combine. Let it simmer for 2 minutes.

STEP 6
Serve warm.

NUTRITIONAL INFORMATION
Calories: 234; Fat: 7 g; Carbs: 32.1 g; Protein: 8.8 g

COCONUT VEGGIE WRAPS

 Cooking Difficulty: 3/10	 Cooking Time: 10 minutes	 Servings: 5

NUTRITIONAL INFORMATION
Calories 236, Carbs 23.6 g, Fats 14.3 g, Protein 5.5 g

INGREDIENTS

- 1½ c. shredded carrots
- 1 red bell pepper, seeded, sliced
- 2½ c. kale
- 1 ripe avocado, sliced
- 1 c. fresh cilantro, chopped
- 5 coconut wraps
- 2/3 c. hummus
- 6½ c. green curry paste

STEP 1

Slice, chop, and shred all the vegetables.

STEP 2

Lay a coconut wrap on a clean flat surface and spread two tablespoons of the hummus and one tablespoon of the green curry paste on top of the end closest to you.

STEP 3

Place some carrots, bell pepper, kale, and cilantro on the wrap and start rolling it up, starting from the edge closest to you. Roll tightly and fold in the ends.

STEP 4

Place the wrap, seam down, on a plate to serve.

TASTY CUCUMBER AVOCADO SANDWICH

INGREDIENTS

- ½ peeled cucumber, sliced
- ¼ tsp. salt
- 4 slices whole-wheat bread
- 4 oz. goat cheese with or without herbs, at room temperature
- 2 romaine lettuce leaves
- 1 pitted avocado, peeled, sliced
- 2 pinches lemon pepper
- 1 squeeze of lemon juice
- ½ c. alfalfa sprouts

NUTRITIONAL INFORMATION
Calories 246, Carbs 20 g, Fats 12 g, Protein 9 g

 Cooking Difficulty: 1/10	 Cooking Time: 15 minutes	 Servings: 2

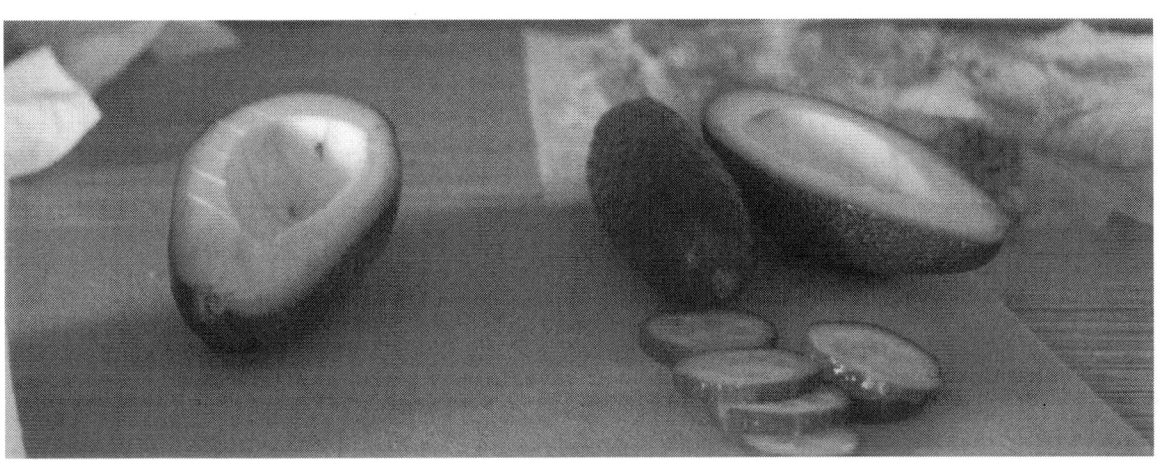

STEP 1
Peel and slice the cucumber thinly. Lay the slices on a plate and sprinkle them with a quarter to a half teaspoon of salt. Let this set for 10 minutes or until water appears on the plate.

STEP 2
Place the cucumber slices in a colander and rinse with cold water. Let these drain, then place them on a dry plate and pat dry with a paper towel.

STEP 3
Spread all slices with goat cheese and place lettuce leaves on the two bottom pieces of bread.

STEP 4
Layer the cucumber slices and avocado atop the bread.

STEP 5
Sprinkle one pinch of lemon pepper over each sandwich and drizzle a little lemon juice over the top.

STEP 6
Top with the alfalfa sprouts and place another piece of bread, goat cheese down, on top.

RICE AND BEAN BURRITOS

 Cooking Difficulty: 3/10	 Cooking Time: 20 minutes	 Servings: 8

INGREDIENTS

- 32 oz. fat-free refried beans
- 6 tortillas
- 2 c. cooked rice
- ½ c. salsa
- 1 tbsp. olive oil
- 1 bunch green onions, chopped
- 2 bell peppers, chopped
- guacamole

STEP 1
Preheat the oven to 375°F.

STEP 2
Dump the refried beans into a saucepan and place over medium heat to warm.

STEP 3
Heat the tortillas and lay them out on a flat surface.

STEP 4
Spoon the beans in a long mound that runs across the tortilla, just a little off from center.

STEP 5
Spoon some rice and salsa over the beans; add the green pepper and onions to taste, along with any other finely chopped vegetables you like.

STEP 6
Fold over the shortest edge of the plain tortilla and roll it up, folding in the sides as you go.

STEP 7
Place each burrito, seam side down, on a nonstick-sprayed baking sheet.

STEP 8
Brush with olive oil and bake for 15 minutes.

STEP 9
Serve with guacamole.

NUTRITIONAL INFORMATION
Calories 290, Carbs 49 g, Fats 6 g, Protein 9 g

LEMON ARTICHOKES

 Cooking Difficulty: 2/10	 Cooking Time: 30 minutes	 Servings: 4

INGREDIENTS

- 1½ c. water
- 2 artichokes
- 1 lemon
- ¼ tsp. salt
- ¼ tsp. pepper
- ¼ tsp. granulated garlic
- 2 tbsps. dijon mustard
- 2 tbsps. olive oil
- 1 lemon wedge

STEP 1
Wash the artichokes well and trim them. Rub them with the lemon wedge.

STEP 2
Pour the water into the Instant Pot and lower the steamer basket.

STEP 3
Place the artichokes in the basket.

STEP 4
Close the lid and cook for 20 minutes on HIGH.

STEP 5
Do a natural pressure release, about 10 minutes. Quickly release the remaining pressure.

STEP 6
In a small bowl, mix together the lemon juice, mustard, olive oil, salt, and pepper.

STEP 7
Serve artichokes with the sauce.

STEP 8
Enjoy!

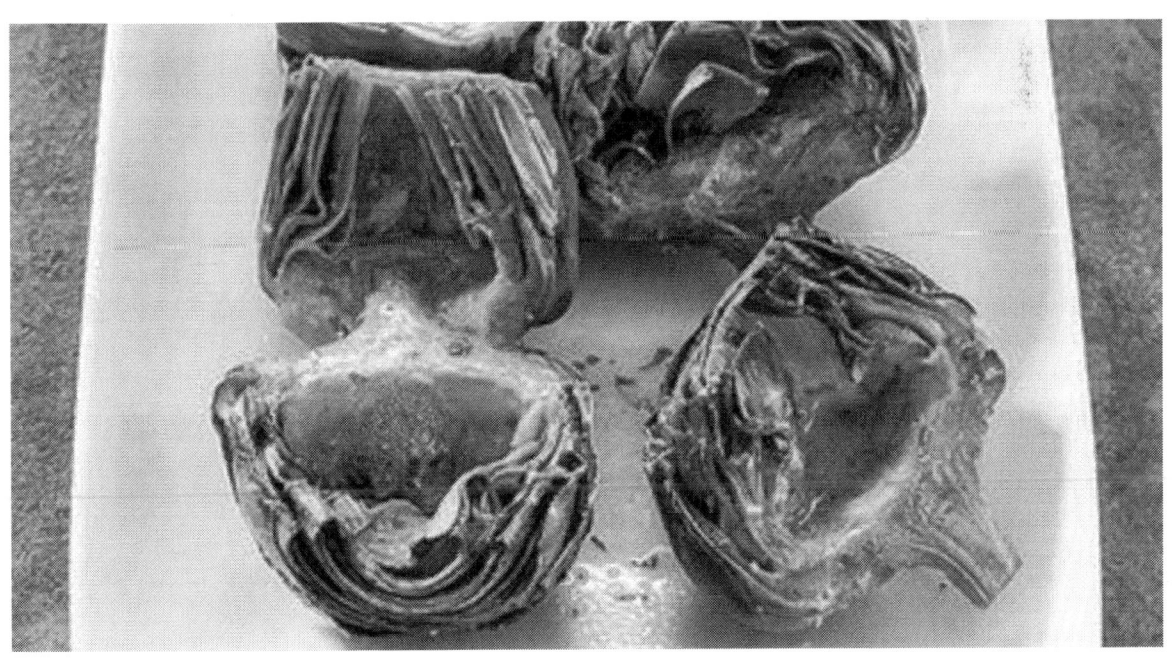

NUTRITIONAL INFORMATION
108 Calories, 7.5g Fat, 5.4g Carbs, 3.1g Protein

SWEET POTATO QUESADILLAS

 Cooking Difficulty: 3/10	 Cooking Time: 80 minutes	 Servings: 3

INGREDIENTS

- 1 c. dry black beans
- ½ c. dry rice of choice
- 1 sweet potato, peeled and diced
- ½ c. salsa
- 4 tortilla wraps
- 1 tbsp. olive oil
- ½ tsp. garlic powder
- ½ tsp. onion powder
- ½ tsp. paprika

NUTRITIONAL INFORMATION
Calories 683, Fat 12.7g, Carbs 121g, Protein 24.9g

STEP 1
Preheat the oven to 350°F.

STEP 2
Line a baking pan with parchment paper.

STEP 3
Cut the sweet potato into ½-inch cubes and drizzle these with olive oil. Transfer the cubes to the baking pan.

STEP 4
In your oven, set in the pan to bake the potatoes until tender, for around 1 hour.

STEP 5
Set aside for 5 minutes for potatoes to cool and then add them to a large mixing bowl with the salsa and cooked rice. Mash well to combine.

STEP 6
Over medium high heat, set your saucepan in place and add the potato/rice mixture, cooked black beans, and spices to the pan.

STEP 7
Cook everything for about 5 minutes or until it is heated through.

STEP 8
Take another frying pan and put it over medium-low heat. Place a tortilla in the pan and fill half of it with a heaping scoop of the potato, bean, and rice mixture.

STEP 9
Fold tortilla in half to ensure the filling is covered and cook the tortilla until both sides are browned—about 4 minutes per side.

STEP 10
Serve the tortillas with some additional salsa on the side.

BARBECUED GREENS & GRITS

 Cooking Difficulty: 5/10

 Cooking Time: 32 minutes

 Servings: 4

INGREDIENTS

- 14 oz. tempeh, sliced
- 3 c. vegetable broth
- 3 c. collard greens, chopped
- ½ c. bbq sauce
- 1 c. gluten-free grits
- ¼ c. white onion, diced
- 2 tbsps. olive oil
- 2 garlic cloves, minced
- 1 tsp. salt

NUTRITIONAL INFORMATION

Calories 374, Fat 19.1g, Carbs 31.1g, Protein 23.7g

STEP 1
Preheat the oven to 400°F.

STEP 2
Mix tempeh slices with the BBQ sauce in a shallow baking dish. Set aside and let marinate for up to 3 hours.

STEP 3
Heat 1 tablespoon of olive oil in a frying pan over medium heat, then add the garlic and sauté until fragrant.

STEP 4
Add the collard greens and ½ teaspoon of salt and cook until the collards are wilted and dark. Set the pan from heat and set aside.

STEP 5
Cover the tempeh and BBQ sauce mixture with aluminum foil. In your oven, set the baking dish in place and bake the ingredients for 15 minutes. Uncover and continue to bake for another 10 minutes until the tempeh is browned and crispy.

STEP 6
While the tempeh cooks heat the remaining tablespoon of olive oil in the previously used frying pan over medium heat.

STEP 7
Cook the onions until brown and fragrant, around 10 minutes.

STEP 8
Pour in the vegetable broth and bring it to a boil; then turn the heat down to low.

STEP 9
Slowly whisk the grits into the simmering broth. Add the remaining ½ teaspoon of salt before covering the pan with a lid.

STEP 10
Let the ingredients simmer for about 8 minutes until the grits are soft and creamy.

STEP 11
Serve the tempeh and collard greens on top of a bowl of grits and enjoy, or store for later!

SWEET POTATO SUSHI

INGREDIENTS

- 14 oz. drained silken tofu
- 4 nori sheets
- 1 peeled sweet potato
- 1 peeled avocado, pitted, sliced
- 1 c. water
- ¾ c. dry sushi rice
- 1 tbsp. rice vinegar
- 1 tbsp. agave nectar
- 1 tbsp. amino acids

 Cooking Difficulty: 5/10

 Cooking Time: 45 minutes

 Servings: 3

NUTRITIONAL INFORMATION

Calories 290, Carbs 39.2 g, Fats 10.3 g, Protein: 10.3 g

STEP 1
Set your oven to 400°F / 200°C.

STEP 2
Stir the amino acids (or tamari) and agave nectar together in a small bowl until it is well combined and then set aside.

STEP 3
Cut the sweet potato into large sticks, around ½-inch thick. Place them on a baking sheet lined with parchment and coat them with the tamari/agave mixture.

STEP 4
Bake sweet potatoes until softened—for about 25 minutes—and make sure to flip them halfway, so the sides cook evenly.

STEP 5
Meanwhile, bring the sushi rice, water, and vinegar to a boil in a medium-sized pot over medium heat, and cook until liquid has evaporated, for about 10 minutes.

STEP 6
While cooking the rice, cut the block of tofu into long sticks. The sticks should look like long, thin fries. Set aside.

STEP 7
Set the pot away from heat and let the rice sit for 10-15 minutes.

STEP 8
Cover your work area with a piece of parchment paper, clean your hands, wet your fingers, and lay out a sheet of nori on the parchment paper.

STEP 9
Cover the nori sheet with a thin layer of sushi rice, while wetting the hands frequently. Leave sufficient space for rolling up the sheet.

STEP 10
Place the roasted sweet potato strips in a straight line across the width of the sheet.

STEP 11
Lay out the tofu and avocado slices right beside the potato sticks and use the parchment paper as an aid to roll up the nori sheet into a tight cylinder.

STEP 12
Slice the cylinder into 8 equal pieces and refrigerate. Repeat for the remaining nori sheets and fillings. Serve chilled, or store to enjoy this delicious sushi later!

COCONUT TOFU CURRY

 Cooking Difficulty: 3/10	 Cooking Time: 20 minutes	 Servings: 2

NUTRITIONAL INFORMATION
Calories 449, Carbs 38.7 g, Fats 23 g, Protein: 21.8 g

INGREDIENTS

- 14 oz. tofu
- 2 tsps. coconut oil
- 1 sweet onion, diced
- 13 oz. reduced-fat coconut milk
- 1 c. fresh tomatoes, diced
- 1 c. snap peas
- 1½ inch ginger, finely minced
- 1 tsp. curry powder
- 1 tsp. turmeric
- 1 tsp. cumin
- ½ tsp. red pepper flakes
- 1 tsp. agave nectar
- salt and pepper

STEP 1
Cut the tofu into ½-inch cubes.

STEP 2
Over n a skillet set over medium-high heat, add coconut oil and heat.

STEP 3
Add the tofu and cook for about 5 minutes.

STEP 4
Stir in the garlic and diced onions, and sauté until the onions are transparent (for about 5 to 10 minutes); add the ginger while stirring.

STEP 5
Add in the coconut milk, tomatoes, agave nectar, snap peas, and remaining spices.

STEP 6
Mix welly, and cook on low heat while covered; remove after 10 minutes of cooking.

STEP 7
For serving, scoop the curry into a bowl or over rice.

STEP 8
Enjoy right away, or store the curry in an airtight container to enjoy later!

CHICKPEA AND SPINACH CUTLETS

INGREDIENTS

- 1 red bell pepper
- 19 oz. chickpeas, rinsed & drained
- 1 c. ground almonds
- 2 tsps. dijon mustard
- 1 tsp. oregano
- ½ tsp. sage
- 1 c. spinach, fresh
- 1½ c. rolled oats
- 1 clove garlic, pressed
- ½ lemon, juiced
- 2 tsps. maple syrup, pure

 Cooking Difficulty: 3/10

 Cooking Time: 40 minutes

 Servings: 12

STEP 1
Get out a baking sheet. Line it with parchment paper.

STEP 2
Cut your red pepper in half and then take the seeds out. Place it on your baking sheet, and roast in the oven while you prepare your other ingredients.

STEP 3
Process your chickpeas, almonds, mustard, and maple syrup together in a food processor.

STEP 4
Add in your lemon juice, oregano, sage, garlic, and spinach, processing again. Make sure it's combined, but don't puree it.

STEP 5
Once your red bell pepper is softened, which should roughly take ten minutes, add this to the processor as well. Add in your oats, mixing well.

STEP 6
Form twelve patties, cooking in the oven for a half hour. They should be browned.

NUTRITIONAL INFORMATION
Calories: 200, Protein: 8 g, Fat: 11g, Carbs: 21 g

BRUSSELS SPROUT SALAD

 Cooking Difficulty: 1/10	 Cooking Time: 5 minutes	 Servings: 4

INGREDIENTS

- 1 lb. Brussels sprouts, trimmed and halved
- 1 c. pomegranate seeds
- ½ c. chopped almonds

STEP 1
Arrange the steamer basket in the bottom of the Instant Pot. Add 1 cup of the water in the Instant Pot.

STEP 2
Arrange the Brussels sprout in steamer basket.

STEP 3
Secure the lid and cook at high pressure for 4 minutes.

STEP 4
When the cooking is complete, carefully do a quick pressure release.

STEP 5
Remove the lid and transfer the Brussels sprouts onto serving plates and drizzle with the melted butter. Top with pomegranate seeds and almonds and serve.

NUTRITIONAL INFORMATION
Calories: 174; Fat: 9.2 g; Carbs: 14.1 g; Protein: 6.7 g

FLAVORFUL REFRIED BEANS

 Cooking Difficulty: 2/10

 Cooking Time: 360 minutes

 Servings: 8

INGREDIENTS

- 3 c. rinsed pinto beans
- 1 seeded jalapeno pepper, chopped
- 1 sliced white onion, peeled
- 2 tbsps. minced garlic
- 5 tsps. salt
- 2 tsps. ground black pepper
- ¼ tsps. ground cumin
- 9 c. water

STEP 1
Using a 6-quarts slow cooker, place all the ingredients and stir until it mixes properly.

STEP 2
Cover the top, plug in the slow cooker, adjust the cooking time to 6 hours, let it cook on high heat setting, and add more water if the beans get too dry.

STEP 3
When beans are done, drain and reserve the liquid.

STEP 4
Use a potato masher to mash the beans and pour in the reserved cooking liquid until it reaches your desired mixture. Serve immediately.

NUTRITIONAL INFORMATION
Calories: 105, Carbs: 36g, Protein:13g, Fats:1g

SMOKY RED BEANS AND RICE

 Cooking Difficulty: 2/10　　 Cooking Time: 365 minutes　　 Servings: 6

INGREDIENTS

- 30 oz. cooked red beans
- 1 c. brown rice, uncooked
- 1 c. green pepper, chopped
- 1 c. chopped celery
- 1 c. white onion, chopped
- 1 ½ tsps. minced garlic
- ½ tsp. salt
- ¼ tsp. cayenne pepper
- 1 tsp. smoked paprika
- 2 tsps. dried thyme
- 1 bay leaf
- 2 1/3 c. vegetable broth

STEP 1
Using a 6-quarts slow cooker, place all the ingredients except for the rice, salt, and cayenne pepper.

STEP 2
Stir until it mixes properly and then cover the top.

STEP 3
Plug in the slow cooker; adjust the cooking time to 4 hours and let it steam on a low heat setting.

STEP 4
Then pour in and stir the rice, salt, cayenne pepper and continue cooking for an additional 2 hours at a high heat setting.

STEP 5
Serve straight away.

NUTRITIONAL INFORMATION
Calories:425 Cal, Carbs:62g, Protein:27g, Fats:22g

SIZZLING VEGETARIAN FAJITAS

 Cooking Difficulty: 2/10	 Cooking Time: 120 minutes	 Servings: 8

INGREDIENTS

- 4 oz. diced green chilies
- 3 diced tomatoes
- 1 cored yellow bell pepper, sliced
- 1 cored red bell pepper, sliced
- 1 white onion, peeled and sliced
- ½ tsp. garlic powder
- ¼ tsp. salt
- 2 tsps. red chili powder
- 2 tsps. ground cumin
- ½ tsp. dried oregano
- 1 ½ tbsps. olive oil

STEP 1
Take a 6-quarts slow cooker, grease it with a non-stick cooking spray, and add all the ingredients.

STEP 2
Stir until it mixes properly and cover the top.

STEP 3
Plug in the slow cooker; adjust the cooking time to 2 hours and let it cook on the high heat setting or until cooks thoroughly.

STEP 4
Serve with tortillas.

NUTRITIONAL INFORMATION
Calories:220 Cal, Carbs:73g, Protein:12g, Fats:8g

RICH RED LENTIL CURRY

 Cooking Difficulty: 3/10	 Cooking Time: 310 minutes	 Servings: 16

INGREDIENTS

- 4 c. uncooked brown lentils, rinsed
- 2 white onions, peeled and diced
- 2 tsps. minced garlic
- 1 tbsp. minced ginger
- 1 tsp. salt
- ¼ tsp. cayenne pepper
- 5 tbsps. red curry paste
- 2 tsps. brown sugar
- 1 ½ tsps. ground turmeric
- 1 tbsp. garam masala
- 60 oz. tomato puree
- 7 c. water
- ½ c. coconut milk
- ¼ c. chopped cilantro

STEP 1
Using a 6-quarts slow cooker, place all the ingredients except for the coconut milk and cilantro.

STEP 2
Stir until it mixes properly and cover the top.

STEP 3
Plug in the slow cooker; adjust the cooking time to 5 hours and let cook on high or until the lentils are soft.

STEP 4
Check the curry during cooking and add more water if needed.

STEP 5
When the curry is cooked, stir in the milk, then garnish it with the cilantro and serve right away.

NUTRITIONAL INFORMATION
Calories:192 Cal, Carbs:33g, Protein:12g, Fats:3g

MASHED CAULIFLOWER

 Cooking Difficulty: 2/10	 Cooking Time: 6 minutes	 Servings: 4

INGREDIENTS

- 1 head cauliflower Head
- 3 tbsps. melt vegetarian butter
- 1 c. water
- ¼ c. pepper
- ½ tsp. salt

STEP 1
Chop the cauliflower and place inside the steamer basket.

STEP 2
Pour the water into the Instant Pot and lower the basket.

STEP 3
Close the lid, set it to MANUAL, and cook at high pressure for 4 minutes.

STEP 4
Do a quick pressure release.

STEP 5
Mash the cauliflower with a potato masher or in a food processor and stir in the remaining ingredients.

STEP 6
Serve and enjoy!

NUTRITIONAL INFORMATION
Calories: 113; Fat: 5.9 g; Carbs: 4.1 g; Protein: 3 g

SAVORY SPANISH RICE

 Cooking Difficulty: 2/10

 Cooking Time: 280 minutes

 Servings: 10

INGREDIENTS

- 1 c. long grain rice, uncooked
- ½ c. green bell pepper, chopped
- 14 oz. diced tomatoes
- ½ c. chopped white onion
- 1 tsp. minced garlic
- ½ tsp. salt
- 1 tsp. red chili powder
- 1 tsp. ground cumin
- 4 oz. tomato puree
- 8 fl. oz. water

STEP 1
Grease a 6-quarts slow cooker with a non-stick cooking spray and add all the ingredients into it.

STEP 2
Stir properly and cover the top.

STEP 3
Plug in the slow cooker; adjust the cooking time to 5 hours and let cook on high or until the rice absorbs all the liquid.

STEP 4
Serve right away.

NUTRITIONAL INFORMATION
Calories:210 Cal, Carbs:11g, Protein:12g, Fats:10g

EXQUISITE BANANA, APPLE, AND COCONUT CURRY

INGREDIENTS

- ½ c. amaranth seeds
- 1 apple, cored and sliced
- 1 banana, sliced
- 1 ½ c. diced tomatoes
- 3 tsps. chopped parsley
- 1 chopped green pepper
- 1 white onion, peeled and diced
- 2 tsps. minced garlic
- 1 tsp. salt
- 1 tsp. ground cumin
- 2 ½ tbsps. curry powder
- 2 tbsps. flour
- 2 bay leaves
- ½ c. white wine
- 8 fl. oz. coconut milk
- ½ c. water

NUTRITIONAL INFORMATION
Calories:370 Cal, Carbs:15g, Protein:5g, Fats:8g

 Cooking Difficulty: 4/10

 Cooking Time: 350 minutes

 Servings: 6

STEP 1
Using a food processor, place the apple, tomatoes, garlic, and pulse it until it gets smooth but a little bit chunky.

STEP 2
Add this mixture to a 6-quarts slow cooker and add the remaining ingredients.

STEP 3
Stir until it mixes properly and cover the top.

STEP 4
Plug in the slow cooker; adjust the cooking time to 6 hours and let it cook on the low heat setting or until it is cooked thoroughly.

STEP 5
Add the seasoning and serve right away.

RAW ZOODLES WITH AVOCADO 'N NUTS

 Cooking Difficulty: 2/10

 Cooking Time: 10 minutes

 Servings: 2

INGREDIENTS

- 1 zucchini
- 1½ c. basil
- 1/3 c. water
- 5 tbsps. pine nuts
- 2 tbsps. lemon juice
- 1 avocado, peeled, pitted, sliced
- optional: 2 tbsps. olive oil
- 6 yellow cherry tomatoes, halved
- optional: 6 red cherry tomatoes, halved
- sea salt and black pepper

STEP 1
Add the basil, water, nuts, lemon juice, avocado slices, optional olive oil (if desired), salt, and pepper to a blender.

STEP 2
Blend the ingredients into a smooth mixture. Season with more pepper and salt and blend again.

STEP 3
Divide the sauce and the zucchini noodles between two medium-sized bowls for serving, and combine in each.

STEP 4
Top the mixtures with the halved yellow cherry tomatoes, and the optional red cherry tomatoes (if desired); serve and enjoy!

NUTRITIONAL INFORMATION
Calories 317, Carbs 7.4 g, Fats 28.1 g, Protein 7.2 g

DELIGHTFUL COCONUT VEGETARIAN CURRY

 Cooking Difficulty: 5/10	 Cooking Time: 300 minutes	 Servings: 6

NUTRITIONAL INFORMATION
Calories:369 Cal, Carbs:39g, Protein:7g, Fats:23g

INGREDIENTS

- 5 potatoes, peeled and cubed
- ¼ c. curry powder
- 2 tbsps. flour
- 1 tbsp. chili powder
- ½ tsp. red pepper flakes
- ½ tsp. cayenne pepper
- 1 green bell pepper, chopped
- 1 red bell pepper, chopped
- 2 tbsps. onion soup mix
- 14 oz. coconut cream, unsweetened
- 3 c. vegetable broth
- 2 carrots, peeled and sliced
- 1 c. green peas
- ¼ c. chopped cilantro

STEP 1
Take a 6-quarts slow cooker, grease it with a non-stick cooking spray and place the potatoes pieces in the bottom.

STEP 2
Set in the rest of the ingredients except for peas, cilantro, and carrots.

STEP 3
Stir properly and cover the top.

STEP 4
Plug in the slow cooker; adjust the cooking time to 4 hours and let it cook on the low heat setting or until it cooks thoroughly.

STEP 5
When the cooking time is over, add the carrots to the curry and continue cooking for 30 minutes.

STEP 6
Stir in the peas to cook for 30 more minutes or until the peas get tender.

STEP 7
Garnish it with cilantro and serve.

CREAMY SWEET POTATO & COCONUT CURRY

 Cooking Difficulty: 6/10

 Cooking Time: 400 minutes

 Servings: 6

INGREDIENTS

- 2 lbs. sweet potatoes, peeled and chopped
- ½ lb. shredded red cabbage
- 2 red chilies, seeded and sliced
- 2 red bell peppers, cored and sliced
- 2 white onions, peeled and sliced
- 1 ½ tsps. minced garlic
- 1 tsp. grated ginger
- ½ tsp. salt
- 1 tsp. paprika
- ½ tsp. cayenne pepper
- 2 tbsps. peanut butter
- 4 tbsps. olive oil
- 12 oz. tomato puree
- 14 fl. oz. coconut milk
- ½ c. chopped coriander

STEP 1
Place a large non-stick skillet pan over an average heat, add 1 tablespoon of oil and let it heat.

STEP 2
Then add the onion and cook for 10 minutes or until it gets soft.

STEP 3
Add the garlic, ginger, salt, paprika, cayenne pepper, and continue cooking for 2 minutes or until it starts producing fragrance.

STEP 4
Transfer this mixture to a 6-quarts slow cooker and reserve the pan.

STEP 5
In the pan, add 1 tablespoon of oil and let it heat.

STEP 6
Add the cabbage, red chili, bell pepper, and cook it for 5 minutes.

STEP 7
Then transfer this mixture to the slow cooker and reserve the pan.

STEP 8
Add the remaining oil to the pan; the sweet potatoes in a single layer and cook it in 3 batches for 5 minutes or until it starts getting brown.

STEP 9
Add the sweet potatoes to the slow cooker, along with tomato puree, coconut milk, and stir properly.

STEP 10
Cover the top, plug in the slow cooker; adjust the cooking time to 6 hours and let cook on low or until the sweet potatoes are tender.

STEP 11
When done, add the seasoning and pour it in the peanut butter.

STEP 12
Garnish it with coriander and serve.

NUTRITIONAL INFORMATION
Calories:434, Carbs:47g, Protein:6g, Fats:22g

BOLOGNESE PASTA

STEP 1
Heat oil in a large-sized saucepan over medium-high heat.

STEP 2
To this, stir in the carrot, celery, shallots, pepper, and salt.

STEP 3
Now, saute the veggies for 2 to 3 minutes or until softened.

STEP 4
Next, spoon in the garlic and cook for further 1 minute or until aromatic.

STEP 5
Then, place the garbanzo beans in the food processor and process them by pulsing them nine times.

STEP 6
After that, spoon in the processed garbanzo beans and marinara sauce to the saucepan. Mix well.

STEP 7
Once combined, pour the oats milk and maple syrup to it. Combine.

STEP 8
Cook for 5 minutes and then lower the heat.

STEP 9
Simmer the mixture for few minutes while keeping it covered with a lid.

STEP 10
Meanwhile, boil a pot of water over medium-high heat.

STEP 11
Add the pasta once the water starts boiling and cook by following the manufacturer's instructions. Cook until al dente.

STEP 12
Finally, stir in the cooked pasta to the sauce mixture and coat well. Garnish with basil and parsley before serving.

 Cooking Difficulty: 3/10	 Cooking Time: 20 minutes	 Servings: 4

INGREDIENTS

- 15 oz. garbanzo beans, drained, washed & dried
- ¼ c. extra virgin olive oil
- ¼ c. parsley, fresh & chopped
- 1 carrot, diced
- 24 oz. marinara sauce
- 1 celery stalk, diced
- 4 garlic cloves, minced
- 8 oz. pasta of your choice
- 1 shallot, diced
- ¼ tsp. black pepper, grounded
- 1 tsp. sea salt
- 2 tsp. maple syrup
- ½ c. oats milk

NUTRITIONAL INFORMATION

Calories: 396, Proteins: 22.4g, Carbs: 55.5g, Fat: 11.5g

COMFORTING CHICKPEA TAGINE

 Cooking Difficulty: 5/10

 Cooking Time: 250 minutes

 Servings: 6

INGREDIENTS

- 14 oz. cooked chickpeas
- 12 dried apricots
- 1 red bell pepper, cored and sliced
- 1 cored butternut squash, peeled and chopped
- 2 stemmed zucchini, chopped
- 1 white onion, peeled and chopped
- 1 tsp. minced garlic
- 1 tsp. ground ginger
- 1 ½ tsps. salt
- 1 tsp. ground black pepper
- 1 tsp. ground cumin
- 2 tsps. paprika
- 1 tsp. harissa paste
- 2 tsps. honey
- 2 tbsps. olive oil
- 1 lb. passata
- ¼ c. chopped coriander

STEP 1
Take a 6-quarts slow cooker, grease it with a non-stick cooking spray and place the chickpeas, apricots, bell pepper, butternut squash, zucchini, and onion into it.

STEP 2
Sprinkle it with salt, black pepper, and set it aside until it is called for.

STEP 3
Place a large non-stick skillet pan over an average temperature of heat; add the oil, garlic, cumin, and paprika.

STEP 4
Stir properly and cook for 1 minutes or until it starts producing fragrance.

STEP 5
Then pour in the harissa paste, honey, passata, and boil the mixture.

STEP 6
When the mixture is done boiling, pour this mixture over the vegetables in the slow cooker and cover it with the lid.

STEP 7
Plug in the slow cooker; adjust the cooking time to 4 hours and let it cook on the high heat setting or until the vegetables gets tender.

STEP 8
When done, add the seasoning, garnish it with the coriander, and serve right away.

NUTRITIONAL INFORMATION
Calories:237, Carbs:45g, Protein:9g, Fats:2g

CAULIFLOWER BOLOGNESE WITH ZUCCHINI NOODLES

INGREDIENTS

- 1 medium head cauliflower, broken into florets
- 2 minced cloves garlic
- ½ c. diced onions
- ¾ tsp. dried basil
- red pepper flakes
- 1 tsp. dried oregano flakes
- ¼ c. vegetable broth
- 1½ cans (14 oz. each) diced tomatoes
- salt
- pepper

for the noodles:
- 4 medium zucchinis

NUTRITIONAL INFORMATION
Calories: 211; Fat: 1.9 g; Carbs: 28.1; Protein: 14.3 g

 Cooking Difficulty: 3/10	 Cooking Time: 7 minutes	 Servings: 2

STEP 1
Add all the ingredients except zucchini to the Instant Pot.

STEP 2
Close the lid. Select MANUAL and cook at high pressure for 3 minutes.

STEP 3
When the cooking is complete, do a quick pressure release.

STEP 4
Meanwhile, make noodles of the zucchini using a spiralizer using blade A or a julienne peeler.

STEP 5
Mash the cauliflower with a potato masher or in a food processor.

STEP 6
Divide the noodles in 4 bowls. Place cauliflower Bolognese over it and serve.

BLACK BEAN AND QUINOA SALAD

 Cooking Difficulty: 2/10

 Cooking Time: 5 minutes

 Servings: 10

INGREDIENTS
- 15 oz. cooked black beans
- 1 chopped red bell pepper, cored
- 1 c. quinoa, cooked
- 1 cored green bell pepper, chopped
- ½ c. vegan feta cheese, crumbled

STEP 1
In a bowl, set in all ingredients, except for cheese, and stir until incorporated.

STEP 2
Top the salad with cheese and serve straight away.

NUTRITIONAL INFORMATION
Calories: 64, Fat: 1 g, Carbs: 8 g, Protein: 3 g

EGGPLANT PARMESAN

INGREDIENTS

- cooking spray
- 2 eggplants, sliced into rounds
- salt and pepper
- 2 tbsps. olive oil
- 1 c. onion, chopped
- 2 cloves garlic, crushed and minced
- 28 oz. crushed tomatoes
- ¼ c. red wine
- 1 tsp. dried basil
- 1 tsp. dried oregano
- ½ c. parmesan cheese
- 1 c. mozzarella cheese
- basil leaves, chopped

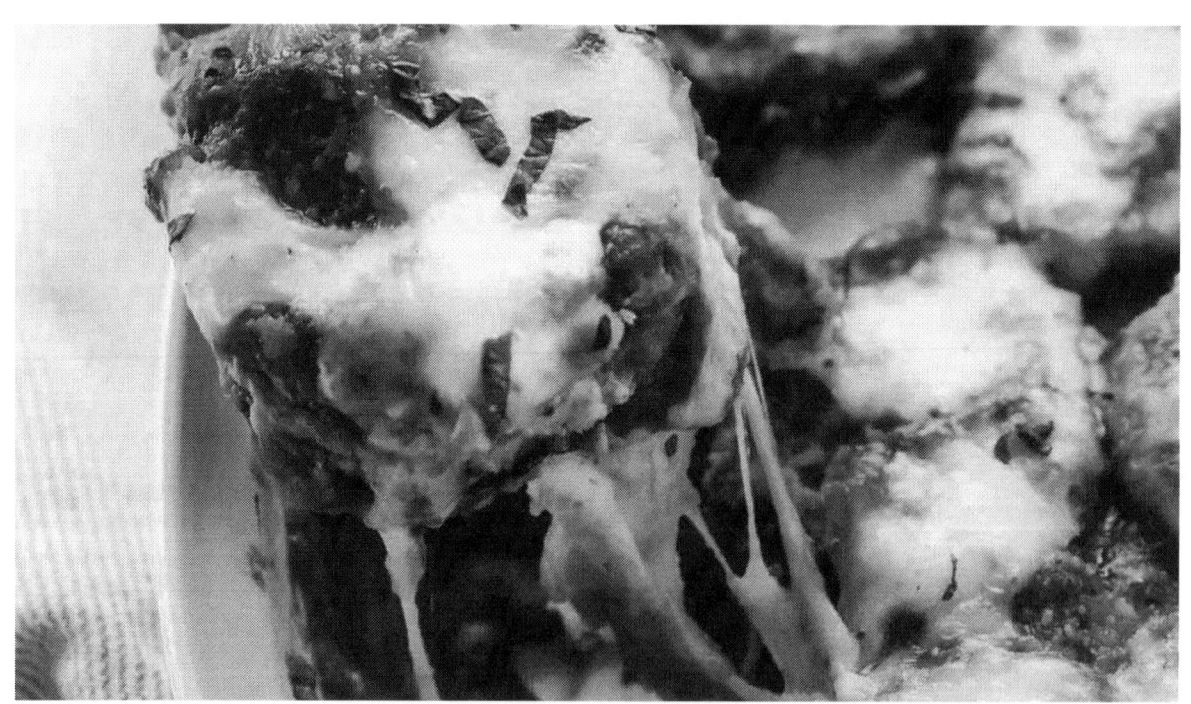

 Cooking Difficulty: 3/10

 Cooking Time: 45 minutes

 Servings: 8

STEP 1
Preheat your oven to 400 degrees f.

STEP 2
Spray your baking pan with oil.

STEP 3
Arrange the eggplant in the baking pan.

STEP 4
Season with salt and pepper.

STEP 5
Roast for 20 minutes.

STEP 6
Over medium heat, set a pan in place. Add the oil and cook the onion for 4 minutes.

STEP 7
Add in garlic and cook for 2 more minutes.

STEP 8
Stir in the rest of the ingredients except the cheese and basil.

STEP 9
Simmer for 10 minutes.

STEP 10
Spread the sauce on a baking dish.

STEP 11
Top with the eggplant slices.

STEP 12
Sprinkle the mozzarella and parmesan on top.

STEP 13
Bake in the oven for 25 minutes.

NUTRITIONAL INFORMATION
Calories 192, Fat 9 g, Carbs 16 g, Protein 10 g

COCONUT CHICKPEA CURRY

 Cooking Difficulty: 4/10

 Cooking Time: 27 minutes

 Servings: 4

NUTRITIONAL INFORMATION
Calories: 225, Fat: 9.4 g, Carbs: 28.5 g, Protein: 7.3

INGREDIENTS

- 2 tsps. coconut flour
- 16 oz. cooked chickpeas
- 14 oz. tomatoes, diced
- 1 red onion, sliced
- 1 ½ tsps. minced garlic
- ½ tsp. sea salt
- 1 tsp. curry powder
- 1/3 tsp. ground black pepper
- 1 ½ tbsps. garam masala
- ¼ tsp. cumin
- 1 lime, juiced
- 13.5 oz. coconut milk, unsweetened
- 2 tbsps. coconut oil

STEP 1

Take a large pot, place it over medium-high heat, add oil and when it melts, add onions and tomatoes, season with salt and black pepper and cook for 5 minutes.

STEP 2

Switch heat to medium-low level, cook for 10 minutes until tomatoes have released their liquid, then add chickpeas and stir in garlic, curry powder, garam masala, and cumin until combined.

STEP 3

Stir in milk and flour, bring the mixture to boil, then switch heat to medium heat and simmer the curry for 12 minutes until cooked.

STEP 4

Taste to adjust seasoning, drizzle with lime juice, and serve.

GREEN BEAN WARM SALAD

 Cooking Difficulty: 3/10

 Cooking Time: 17 minutes

 Servings: 3

INGREDIENTS

- ½ oz. dry porcini mushrooms
- 1 lb. potatoes, peeled, cut into 1-inch chunks
- 1 lb. fresh green beans, trimmed and chopped
- ½ tsp. salt, divided
- 1 c. boiling water

STEP 1
Place mushrooms in a bowl. Pour boiling water over it. Cover and set aside for 5 minutes.

STEP 2
Add mushrooms along with the water into the Instant Pot. Place potatoes over it. Sprinkle with half the salt.

STEP 3
Place a steamer basket over the potatoes and place green beans on the steamer basket. Sprinkle the remaining salt over it.

STEP 4
Close the lid. Select MANUAL and cook at high pressure for 5 minutes.

STEP 5
When the cooking is complete, do a natural pressure release for 5 minutes. Quick release the remaining pressure.

STEP 6
Transfer the beans, potatoes, and mushrooms along with the cooked liquid into a serving bowl. Toss well.

STEP 7
Add your favorite seasonings and serve.

NUTRITIONAL INFORMATION
Calories: 169; Fat: 0.3 g; Carbs: 26.9; Protein: 6.5 g

SUN-DRIED TOMATO PESTO PASTA

 Cooking Difficulty: 2/10

 Cooking Time: 11 minutes

 Servings: 5

INGREDIENTS

- 1 c. fresh basil leaves
- 6 oz. sun-dried tomatoes
- 1 tbsp. lemon juice
- ½ tsp. salt
- ¼ c. olive oil
- ¼ c. almonds
- 3 minced garlic cloves
- ½ tsp. chopped red pepper flakes
- 8 oz. pasta

STEP 1
Cook the pasta according to the given instructions. For making, the pesto toasts the almonds over medium flame in a small skillet for around 4 minutes.

STEP 2
In a blender, put sun-dried tomatoes, basil, garlic, lemon juice, salt, red pepper flakes, and toasted almonds and blend it. While blending adds olive oil in it and blend it until it converts in the form of a pesto.

STEP 3
Now coat the pasta with the pesto and serve it.

NUTRITIONAL INFORMATION
Calories 256, Fat 13.7g, Carbs 28.1g, Protein 6.7g

CAULIFLOWER STEAK WITH SWEET-PEA PUREE

 Cooking Difficulty: 3/10	 Cooking Time: 35 minutes	 Servings: 2

NUTRITIONAL INFORMATION
Calories 234, Fat 3.8g, Carbs 40.3g, Protein 14.5g

INGREDIENTS

Cauliflower:
- 2 heads cauliflower
- 1 tsp. olive oil
- ¼ tsp. paprika
- 1 tsp. coriander
- ¼ tsp. black pepper

Sweet-pea puree:
- 10 oz. frozen green peas
- 1 onion, chopped
- 2 tbsps. fresh parsley
- ¼ c. unsweetened soy milk

STEP 1
Preheat oven to 425F.

STEP 2
Remove bottom core of cauliflower. Stand it on its base, starting in the middle, slice in half. Then slice steaks about ¾ inches thick.

STEP 3
Using a baking pan, set in the steaks.

STEP 4
Using olive oil, coat the front and back of the steaks.

STEP 5
Sprinkle with coriander, paprika, and pepper.

STEP 6
Bake for 30 minutes, flipping once.

STEP 7
Meanwhile, steam the chopped onion and peas until soft.

STEP 8
Place these vegetables in a blender with milk and parsley and blend until smooth.

SPINACH AND MASHED TOFU SALAD

 Cooking Difficulty: 2/10

 Cooking Time: 8 minutes

 Servings: 4

INGREDIENTS

- 16 oz. blocks firm tofu, drained
- 4 c. baby spinach leaves
- 4 tbsps. cashew butter
- 1½ tbsps. soy sauce
- 1-inch piece ginger, chopped
- 1 tsp. red miso paste
- 2 tbsps. sesame seeds
- 1 tsp. organic orange zest
- 1 tsp. nori flakes
- 2 tbsps. water

STEP 1
Dry excess water left in the tofu using a paper towel before crumbling both blocks into small pieces.

STEP 2
In a large bowl, combine the mashed tofu with the spinach leaves.

STEP 3
Mix the remaining ingredients in another small bowl and, if desired, add the optional water for a more smooth dressing.

STEP 4
Pour this dressing over the mashed tofu and spinach leaves.

STEP 5
Allow the salad to chill for up to one hour. Doing so will guarantee a better flavor. Or, the salad can be served right away. Enjoy!

NUTRITIONAL INFORMATION
Calories 166, Carbs 5.5 g, Fats 10.7 g, Protein 11.3 g

SWEET POTATO AND WHITE BEAN SKILLET

 Cooking Difficulty: 4/10　 Cooking Time: 30 minutes　 Servings: 4

NUTRITIONAL INFORMATION
Calories: 263, Fat: 4 g, Carbs: 44 g, Protein: 13 g

INGREDIENTS

- 1 bunch kale, chopped
- 2 sweet potatoes, peeled, cubed
- 12 oz. cannellini beans
- 1 peeled onion, diced
- 1/8 tsp. red pepper flakes
- 1 tsp. salt
- 1 tsp. cumin
- ½ tsp. ground black pepper
- 1 tsp. curry powder
- 1 ½ tbsps. coconut oil
- 6 oz. coconut milk, unsweetened

STEP 1
Take a large skillet pan, place it over medium heat, add ½ tablespoon oil and when it melts, add onion and cook for 5 minutes.

STEP 2
Then stir in sweet potatoes, stir well, cook for 5 minutes, then season with all the spices, cook for 1 minute and remove the pan from heat.

STEP 3
Take another pan, add remaining oil in it, place it over medium heat and when oil melts, add kale, season with some salt and black pepper, stir well, pour in the milk and cook for 15 minutes until tender.

STEP 4
Then add beans, beans, and red pepper, stir until mixed and cook for 5 minutes until hot.

STEP 5
Serve straight away.

SPICED OKRA

 Cooking Difficulty: 3/10	 Cooking Time: 8 minutes	 Servings: 4

INGREDIENTS

- 2 tbsps. olive oil
- 6 chopped garlic cloves
- 1 tsp. cumin seeds
- 2 sliced onions
- 2 chopped tomatoes
- 2 lbs. okra, cut into 1-inch pieces
- ½ c. vegetable broth
- 1 tsp. ground coriander
- ½ tsp. red chili powder
- ½ tsp. ground turmeric
- Salt
- Pepper

STEP 1
Place the oil in the Instant Pot and select SAUTÉ. Add the garlic and cumin seeds and cook for 1 minute.

STEP 2
Add the onion and cook for 4 minutes.

STEP 3
Add the remaining ingredients and cook for 1 more minute.

STEP 4
Press CANCEL and stir well.

STEP 5
Secure the lid and cook at high pressure for 2 minutes.

STEP 6
When the cooking is complete, do a quick pressure release. Serve hot. .

NUTRITIONAL INFORMATION
Calories: 195; Fat: 7.8 g; Carbs: 17 g; Protein: 6 g

BALSAMIC-GLAZED ROASTED CAULIFLOWER

 Cooking Difficulty: 3/10	 Cooking Time: 75 minutes	 Servings: 4

INGREDIENTS

- 1 head cauliflower
- ½ lb. green beans, trimmed
- 1 peeled red onion, wedged
- 2 c. cherry tomatoes
- ½ tsp. salt
- ¼ c. brown sugar
- 3 tbsps. olive oil
- 1 c. balsamic vinegar
- 2 tbsps. chopped parsley, for garnish

STEP 1
Place cauliflower florets in a baking dish, add tomatoes, green beans, and onion wedges around it, season with salt, and drizzle with oil.

STEP 2
Pour vinegar in a saucepan, stir in sugar, bring the mixture to a boil and simmer for 15 minutes until reduced by half.

STEP 3
Brush the sauce generously over cauliflower florets and then roast for 1 hour at 400 degrees f until cooked, brushing sauce frequently.

STEP 4
When done, garnish vegetables with parsley and then serve.

NUTRITIONAL INFORMATION
Calories: 86, Fat: 5.7 g, Carbs: 7.7 g, Protein: 3.1 g

ASIAN BRUSSELS SPROUTS

 Cooking Difficulty: 2/10

 Cooking Time: 6 minutes

 Servings: 4

INGREDIENTS

- 1 lb. halved brussels sprouts
- 3 tbsps. vegetable stock
- salt
- black pepper
- 1 tsp. toasted sesame seeds
- 1½ tbsps. stevia
- 1 tbsp. coconut aminos
- 2 tbsp. olive oil
- 1 tbsp. sriracha sauce

STEP 1
In a bowl, mix oil with coconut aminos, sriracha, stevia, salt, and black pepper and whisk well.

STEP 2
Put Brussels sprouts in your instant pot, add sriracha mix, stock and sesame seeds, stir, cover and cook on High for 4 minutes.

STEP 3
Serve and enjoy!

NUTRITIONAL INFORMATION
110 Calories, 4 g Fat, 4g Carbs, 2g Protein

CARROT CASHEW PATE

 Cooking Difficulty: 1/10
 Cooking Time: 4 minutes
 Servings: 4

INGREDIENTS

- 2 c. carrots, chopped
- 1 c. cashews, soaked
- ¼ c. tahini
- ¼ c. lemon juice
- 1 tbsp. peeled and grated ginger
- ½ cilantro stems and leaves
- ½ tsp. salt

STEP 1
In a food processor, add in carrots to blend well and ensure no big chunks are present.

STEP 2
Drain cashews and add into the processor with tahini, lemon juice, ginger, cilantro, and salt.

STEP 3
Process until completely smooth. Add salt to taste. Serve.

NUTRITIONAL INFORMATION
Calories 318, Fat 24.2g, carbs 21.3g, Protein 8.6g

LINGUINE WITH WILD MUSHROOMS

 Cooking Difficulty: 2/10

 Cooking Time: 10 minutes

 Servings: 4

INGREDIENTS

- 12 oz. mixed mushrooms, sliced
- 2 green onions, sliced
- 1 ½ tsps. minced garlic
- 1 lb. whole-grain linguine pasta, cooked
- ¼ c. nutritional yeast
- ½ tsp. salt
- ¾ tsp. ground black pepper
- 6 tbsps. olive oil
- ¾ c. vegetable stock, hot

STEP 1
Take a skillet pan, place it over medium-high heat, add garlic and mushroom and cook for 5 minutes until tender.

STEP 2
Transfer the vegetables to a pot, add pasta and remaining ingredients, except for green onions, toss until combined and cook for 3 minutes until hot.

STEP 3
Garnish with green onions and serve.

NUTRITIONAL INFORMATION
Calories: 430, Fat: 15 g, Carbs: 62 g, Protein: 15 g

TOMATO WITH TOFU

 Cooking Difficulty: 1/10	 Cooking Time: 5 minutes	 Servings: 4

INGREDIENTS

- 1 c. diced tomatoes
- 1 cubed block firm tofu
- ½ c. vegetable broth
- 2 tsps. italian seasoning
- 2 tbsps. jarred banana pepper rings
- 1 tbsp. olive oil
- green onions
- dried basil optional

STEP 1
Place all of the ingredients in the Instant Pot. Stir to combine the mixture well.

STEP 2
Close the lid and hit MANUAL. Cook for 4 minutes on HIGH.

STEP 3
Do a quick pressure release. Serve and enjoy!

NUTRITIONAL INFORMATION
68 Calories, 5.4g Fat, 2.3g Carbs, 2.9g Protein

173

EDAMAME AND NOODLE SALAD

 Cooking Difficulty: 3/10

 Cooking Time: 5 minutes

 Servings: 4

INGREDIENTS

- 24 oz. shirataki noodles
- 1 apple, sliced
- 2 c. grape tomatoes halved
- 3 c. frozen edamame shelled
- 3 c. shredded carrots
- 2 c. frozen corn
- ½ tsp. salt
- ½ c. rice vinegar
- 1 tbsp. sriracha hot sauce and more for serving
- ½ c. peanut butter
- 2 tbsps. water
- ½ c. cilantro, chopped

STEP 1
Take a large pot, place it over high heat, pour in water, bring it to boil, then add noodles, corn, and edamame, boil for 2 minutes and drain when done.

STEP 2
Place remaining ingredients in a large bowl, whisk until combined, then add boiled vegetables and toss until well coated.

STEP 3
Drizzle with more sriracha sauce and toss until combined.

NUTRITIONAL INFORMATION
Calories: 455, Fat: 22 g, Carbs: 50 g, Protein: 22 g

PILAF WITH GARBANZOS AND DRIED APRICOTS

INGREDIENTS

- 1 c. bulgur
- 6 oz. cooked chickpeas
- ½ c. dried apricot
- 1 white onion, peeled, diced
- ½ tsps. minced garlic
- 2 tsps. curry powder
- ½ tsp. salt
- 1 tbsp. olive oil
- ¼ c. fresh parsley leaves
- 2 c. vegetable broth
- ¾ c. water

NUTRITIONAL INFORMATION

Calories: 222, Fat: 4.5 g, Carbs: 35 g, Protein: 9.5 g

 Cooking Difficulty: 3/10
 Cooking Time: 15 minutes
 Servings: 4

STEP 1
Take a saucepan, place it over high heat, pour in water and 1 ½ cup broth, and bring it to a boil.

STEP 2
Then stir in bulgur, switch heat to medium-low level and simmer for 15 minutes until most of the liquid has absorbed.

STEP 3
Meanwhile, take a skillet pan, place it over medium heat, add oil and when hot, add onion, cook for 10 minutes, then stir in garlic and curry powder and cook for another minute.

STEP 4
Then add apricots, beans, and salt, pour in remaining broth and bring the mixture to boiling.

STEP 5
Remove pan from heat, fluff the bulgur with a fork, add to the onion-apricot mixture and stir until mixed.

STEP 6
Garnish with parsley and serve.

VEGGIE KABOBS

 Cooking Difficulty: 3/10	 Cooking Time: 15 minutes	 Servings: 10

NUTRITIONAL INFORMATION
Calories: 110, Fat: 9 g, Carbs: 8 g, Protein: 3 g

INGREDIENTS

- 8 oz. button mushrooms, halved
- 2 lbs. summer squash, peeled, 1-inch cubed
- 12 oz. small broccoli florets
- 2 c. grape tomatoes
- 1 tsp. salt
- ½ tsp. smoked paprika
- 1 tsp. ground cumin
- 6 tbsps. olive oil
- 1/2 tsp. ground coriander
- 1 lime, juiced

STEP 1
Toss broccoli florets with 1 tablespoon oil, toss tomatoes and squash pieces with 2 tablespoons oil, then toss mushrooms with 1 tablespoon oil and thread these vegetables onto skewers.

STEP 2
Grill mushrooms and broccoli for 7 to 10 minutes, squash and tomatoes and 8 minutes, and when done, transfer the skewers to a plate and drizzle with lime juice and remaining oil.

STEP 3
Prepared the spice mix and for this, stir together salt, paprika, cumin, and coriander, sprinkle half of the mixture over grilled veggies, cover them with foil for 5 minutes, and then sprinkle with the remaining spice mix.

STEP 4
Serve straight away.

SPAGHETTI WITH CHICKPEAS MEATBALLS

 Cooking Difficulty: 4/10

 Cooking Time: 40 minutes

 Servings: 8

INGREDIENTS

- ½ c. breadcrumbs
- 1 tsp. italian seasoning
- 3 c. chickpeas, drained & rinsed
- ½ tsp. salt
- 3 tbsps. flax seed, grounded
- 2 tsps. onion powder
- 8 tbsps. water
- ½ tbsp. garlic powder
- ¼ c. nutritional yeast
- for the pasta:
- 1 lb. spaghetti
- 25 oz. pasta sauce

STEP 1
First, preheat the oven to 325 °F.

STEP 2
After that, combine the flax seeds with water in a small bowl and set it aside for 5 minutes.

STEP 3
Next, place the chickpeas and salt in the food processor and process them for one minute or until you get a smooth mixture.

STEP 4
Now, transfer the chickpea mixture and the flaxseed mixture to a large mixing bowl. Stir well.

STEP 5
Once combined, add all the remaining ingredients needed to the bowl.

STEP 6
Give everything a good stir and mix well.

STEP 7
Then, make balls out of this mixture and arrange them on a parchment paper-lined baking sheet while leaving ample space in between.

STEP 8
Bake them for 33 to 35 minutes. Turn them once halfway through.

STEP 9
In the meantime, make the spaghetti by following the instructions given on the packet. Cook until al dente.

STEP 10
Finally, place the spaghetti on the serving plate and top it with the meatballs and pasta sauce.

STEP 11
Serve and enjoy.

NUTRITIONAL INFORMATION
Calories: 323, Proteins: 15g, Carbs: 63g, Fat: 4g

APPLE LENTIL SALAD

INGREDIENTS

- 2 c. lentil, dried
- ½ c. pepitas, roasted
- 1 tsp. salt
- 2 celery stalks, chopped
- 2 apples, chopped
- ¼ c. cranberries, dried
- 1 tbsp. rosemary, fresh & chopped
- 1 tbsp. lemon juice
- 2 tbsps. parsley, chopped
- dressing of your choice

NUTRITIONAL INFORMATION

Calories: 431, Proteins: 26.5g, Carbs: 75.2g, Fat: 3.3g

 Cooking Difficulty: 4/10	 Cooking Time: 30 minutes	 Servings: 4

STEP 1
To start with, cook the lentils by following the instructions given in the packet until they are tender.

STEP 2
Once cooked, allow them to cool and place them in the refrigerator until used.

STEP 3
Next, mix the apples with lemon juice in a bowl. Keep it in the refrigerator.

STEP 4
After that, combine the chopped apples with the lentils and the remaining ingredients in the bowl.

STEP 5
Now, drizzle the dressing of your choice and place it in the refrigerator for at least an hour before serving.

STEP 6
Serve and enjoy.

BEET SALAD

STEP 1
Arrange the trivet in the Instant Pot. Add 1 cup of water in the Instant Pot.

STEP 2
Place the beets on top of trivet in a single layer.

STEP 3
Secure the lid and cook at high pressure for 20 minutes.

STEP 4
When the cooking is complete, do a quick pressure release.

STEP 5
Remove the inner pot and rinse the beet under running cold water.

STEP 6
Cut the beets in desired size slices and transfer into a salad bowl.

STEP 7
Add spinach and drizzle with vinegar.

STEP 8
In a bowl, add all dressing ingredients and beat until well combined.

STEP 9
Pour dressing over beets mixture and gently toss to coat well.

STEP 10
Serve with the topping of cheese.

 Cooking Difficulty: 2/10	 Cooking Time: 25 minutes	 Servings: 4

INGREDIENTS

- 8 trimmed beets
- 4 c. fresh baby spinach
- 2 tbsps. balsamic vinegar
- 2 tbsps. tofu cheese

For Dressing:
- 4 tbsps. capers
- 1 minced garlic clove
- 2 tbsps. freshly minced parsley
- 2 tbsps. extra-virgin olive oil
- Salt
- Pepper

NUTRITIONAL INFORMATION

Calories: 174; Fat: 8.6g; Carbs: 17.3 g; Protein: 5.3 g

QUINOA EDAMAME SALAD

 Cooking Difficulty: 3/10	 Cooking Time: 25 minutes	 Servings: 4

NUTRITIONAL INFORMATION
Calories: 295, Proteins: 7.6g, Carbs: 18.7g, Fat: 22.9g

INGREDIENTS

- 1 c. corn, frozen
- 1/8 tsp. black pepper, grounded
- 2 c. edamame shelled & frozen
- ¼ tsp. chilli powder
- 1 c. quinoa, cooked & cooled
- 1 tbsp. lime juice, fresh
- 1 green onion, sliced
- ¼ tsp. thyme, dried
- 2 tbsps. cilantro, fresh & chopped
- ¼ tsp. salt
- ½ red bell pepper, chopped
- 1 tbsp. lemon juice
- pinch of cayenne pepper
- 1 ½ tbsps. olive oil

STEP 1
Heat water in a large pot over medium heat.

STEP 2
To this, stir in the edamame and corn.

STEP 3
Boil them slightly and cook them until they are tender.

STEP 4
Once cooked, drain the water and set it aside.

STEP 5
Now, combine all the remaining veggies and quinoa in a large bowl along with the cooked corn and edamame. Toss well.

STEP 6
In the meantime, to make the dressing, mix olive oil, lemon juice, lime juice, black pepper, thyme, chilli powder, and cayenne until emulsified.

STEP 7
Next, drizzle the dressing over the salad and place it in the refrigerator for at least 2 hours. Serve and enjoy.

CABBAGE WITH CARROT

INGREDIENTS

- 2 tbsps. coconut oil
- 2 sliced onions
- salt
- 2 chopped garlic cloves
- 1 jalapeño pepper, seeded and chopped
- 1 tbsp. mild curry powder
- 1 head cabbage, shredded
- 2 carrots, peeled and sliced
- ½ c. desiccated unsweetened coconut
- 2 tbsps. fresh lemon juice
- 1 c. water

NUTRITIONAL INFORMATION

Calories: 185; Fat: 10.7g; Carbs: 13.6g; Protein: 4.3g

 Cooking Difficulty: 4/10	 Cooking Time: 30 minutes	 Servings: 4

STEP 1
Place the coconut oil in the Instant Pot and select SAUTÉ. Add the onion and salt and cook for 4 minutes.

STEP 2
Add the garlic, jalapeño and curry powder and cook for 1 minute.
Press CANCEL and stir in remaining ingredients.

STEP 3
Press CANCEL and stir in remaining ingredients.

STEP 4
Secure the lid and cook at high pressure for 5 minutes.

STEP 5
When the cooking is complete, do a natural pressure release for 5 minutes. Quick release the remaining pressure.

STEP 6
Serve warm.

BLACK BEAN WRAP WITH HUMMUS

STEP 1
First, preheat the oven to 450 °F.

STEP 2
Next, spoon in oil to a heated skillet and stir in the onion.

STEP 3
Cook them for 2 to 3 minutes or until softened.

STEP 4
After that, stir in the bell pepper and saute for another 3 minutes.

STEP 5
Then, add mushrooms and corn to the skillet. Saute for 2 minutes.

STEP 6
In the meantime, spread the hummus over the wraps.

STEP 7
Now, place the sautéed vegetables, spinach, poblano strips, and beans.

STEP 8
Roll them into a burrito and place on a baking sheet with the seam side down.

STEP 9
Finally, bake them for 9 to 10 minutes.

STEP 10
Serve them warm.

 Cooking Difficulty: 4/10	 Cooking Time: 16 minutes	 Servings: 2

INGREDIENTS

- 1 poblano pepper, roasted
- ½ packet spinach
- 1 onion, chopped
- 2 whole grain wraps
- ½ can black beans
- 1 bell pepper, seeded & chopped
- 4 oz. mushrooms, sliced
- ½ c. corn
- 8 oz. red bell pepper hummus, roasted

NUTRITIONAL INFORMATION

Calories: 293, Proteins: 13.7g, Carbs: 42.8g, Fat: 8.8g

SNACKS AND DESSERTS

BAKED CARROT CHIPS

 Cooking Difficulty: 2/10	 Cooking Time: 15 minutes	 Servings: 8

NUTRITIONAL INFORMATION
Calories: 100, Carbs: 12g, Fats: 8g, Proteins: 1g

INGREDIENTS

- ¼ c. olive oil
- 1 tsp. ground cinnamon
- 1 tsp. ground cumin
- salt
- 3 lbs. carrots

STEP 1

Heating your oven to 425 and setting up a baking sheet with some parchment paper.

STEP 2

Next, you will want to chop the top off each carrot and slice the carrot up paper-thin. You can complete this task by using a knife, but it typically is easier if you have a mandolin slicer.

STEP 3

Toss them in a small bowl with the cinnamon, cumin, olive oil, and a touch of salt. When the carrot slices are well coated, go ahead and lay them across your baking sheet.

STEP 4

Finally, pop the carrots into the oven for fifteen minutes. After this time, you may notice that the edges are going to start to curl and get crispy. At this point, remove the dish from the oven and flip all of the chips over. Return the dish into the oven for six or seven minutes, and then your chips will be set!

BROWNIE ENERGY BITES

 Cooking Difficulty: 2/10	 Cooking Time: 7 minutes	 Servings: 2

INGREDIENTS

- ½ c. walnuts
- 1 c. chopped Medjool dates
- ½ c. almonds
- 1/8 tsp. salt
- ½ c. shredded coconut flakes
- 1/3 c. and 2 tsps. cocoa powder, unsweetened

STEP 1
Using a foode processore, set in walnuts and almonds to pulse for 3 minutes until the dough starts to come together.

STEP 2
Add remaining ingredients, reserving ¼ cup of coconut and pulse for 2 minutes until incorporated.

STEP 3
Shape the mixture into balls, roll them in remaining coconut until coated, and refrigerate for 1 hour.

STEP 4
Serve straight away.

NUTRITIONAL INFORMATION
Calories: 174.6, Fat: 8.1 g, Carbs: 25.5 g, Protein: 4.1 g

PICKLED CUCUMBER SALAD

 Cooking Difficulty: 2/10

 Cooking Time: 17 minutes

 Servings: 2

INGREDIENTS

- 1 sliced cucumber
- ¼ c. rice wine vinegar
- 2 sliced onions
- 1 minced dill
- 1 tsp. sugar
- Salt
- Pepper

STEP 1
Put onions and sliced cucumber inside the Instant Pot Pressure Cooker. Pour white wine vinegar and dill. Season with sugar, salt, and pepper. Mix well.

STEP 2
Close the lid. Lock in place and make sure to seal the valve. Press the "manual" button and cook for 5 minutes on high.

STEP 3
When the timer beeps, choose the quick pressure release. This would take 1–2 minutes. Remove the lid.

STEP 4
Transfer mixture into a bowl. Refrigerate for 10 minutes before serving.

NUTRITIONAL INFORMATION
Calories: 67.5; Fat: 7.1g; Carbs: 16.9g; Protein: 1.3g

CHILI ASPARAGUS

 Cooking Difficulty: 2/10	 Cooking Time: 128 minutes	 Servings: 2

INGREDIENTS

- 1 bundle asparagus
- 1 diced red chili
- ½ tsp. cumin seeds
- 1 tbsp. fresh coriander
- 3 tbsps. olive oil
- ½ of lime juice
- salt
- pepper

NUTRITIONAL INFORMATION

Calories: 440; Fat: 74g; Carbs: 34g; Protein: 9g

STEP 1
Put together chili, lime juice, olive oil, cumin, and coriander in a mixing bowl. Mix well.

STEP 2
Transfer the mixture into a cling film and roll. Put inside the refrigerator for 1–2 hours.

STEP 3
Meanwhile, place the asparagus in the Instant Pot Pressure Cooker. Drizzle in olive oil. Close the lid carefully. Press the "slow cook" button and cook for 2 hours.

STEP 4
When the timer beeps, choose the quick pressure release. This would take 1–2 minutes. Remove the lid.

STEP 5
Turn off the pressure cooker. Carefully remove the lid.

STEP 6
Transfer asparagus in a platter. Spread the chili mixture on top of the asparagus. Serve.

SWEET CINNAMON CHIPS

 Cooking Difficulty: 1/10

 Cooking Time: 4 minutes

 Servings: 5

INGREDIENTS

- 10 whole wheat tortillas
- 1 tsp. ground cinnamon
- 3 tbsps. sugar
- 2 c. olive oil

STEP 1
Getting out a small bowl so you can mix the cinnamon and sugar together. When this is complete, set it to the side.

STEP 2
Next, get out your frying pan and bring the olive oil to a soft simmer. While the oil gets to a simmer, take some time to slice your tortillas up into wedges. When these are set, carefully place them into your simmering olive oil and cook for about two minutes on each side, or until golden.

STEP 3
Once the chips are all set, pat them down with a paper towel and then generously coat each chip with the cinnamon mixture you made earlier. After that, your chips will be set for your enjoyment.

NUTRITIONAL INFORMATION
Calories: 70, Carbs: 5g, Fats: 5g, Proteins: 1g

CAULIFLOWER POPCORN

 Cooking Difficulty: 1/10	 Cooking Time: 480 minutes	 Servings: 4

INGREDIENTS

- 2 tbsps. olive oil
- 2 tsps. chili powder
- 2 tsps. cumin
- 1 tbsp. nutritional yeast
- 1 head cauliflower
- salt

STEP 1
Before you begin making this recipe, you will want to take a few moments to cut your cauliflower into bite-sized pieces, like popcorn.

STEP 2
Once your cauliflower is set, place it into a mixing bowl and coat with the olive oil. Once coated properly, add in the nutritional yeast, salt, and the rest of the spices.

STEP 3
You can enjoy your snack immediately or place into a dehydrator at 115 for 8 hours. By doing this, it will make the cauliflower crispy! You can really enjoy it either way.

NUTRITIONAL INFORMATION
Calories: 100, Carbs: 10g, Fats: 5g, Proteins: 5g

GARLICKY BELL PEPPERS

 Cooking Difficulty: 2/10	 Cooking Time: 5 minutes	 Servings: 4

NUTRITIONAL INFORMATION
Calories: 149; Fat: 7.7g; Carbs: 17 g; Protein: 2.9g

INGREDIENTS

- 2 tbsps. olive oil
- 8 minced garlic cloves
- 2 jalapeño peppers, seeded and chopped
- 2 green bell peppers, seeded and chopped
- 2 red bell peppers, seeded and chopped
- 2 yellow bell peppers, seeded and chopped
- 2 orange bell pepper, seeded and chopped
- salt
- pepper
- ½ c. water
- 2 tbsps. fresh lemon juice

STEP 1
Place the oil in the Instant Pot and select SAUTÉ. Add the garlic and jalapeño and cook for 1 minute.

STEP 2
Press CANCEL and stir in remaining ingredients, except lemon juice.

STEP 3
Secure the lid and cook at high pressure for 2 minutes.

STEP 4
When the cooking is complete, use a quick pressure release.

STEP 5
Remove the lid and select SAUTÉ.

STEP 6
Stir in lemon juice and cook for 1–2 minutes.

STEP 7
Press CANCEL and serve.

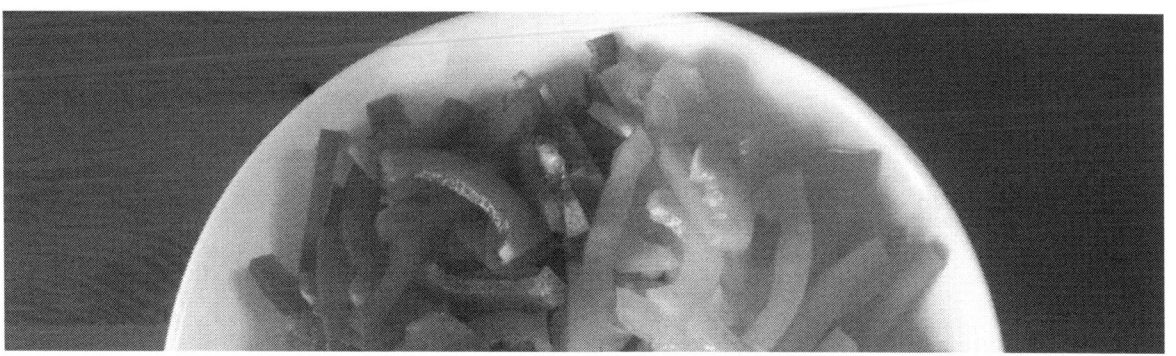

RAINBOW FRUIT SALAD

 Cooking Difficulty: 1/10	 Cooking Time: 5 minutes	 Servings: 4

INGREDIENTS

For the Fruit Salad:
- 1 lb. hulled strawberries, sliced
- 1 c. kiwis, halved, cubed
- 1 ¼ c. blueberries
- 1 1/3 c. blackberries
- 1 c. pineapple chunks

For the Maple Lime Dressing:
- 2 tsps. lime zest
- ¼ c. maple syrup
- 1 tbsp. lime juice

STEP 1
Prepare the salad, and for this, take a bowl, place all its ingredients and toss until mixed.

STEP 2
Prepare the dressing, and for this, take a small bowl, place all its ingredients and whisk well.

STEP 3
Drizzle the dressing over salad, toss until coated and serve.

NUTRITIONAL INFORMATION
Calories: 88.1, Fat: 0.4 g, Carbs: 22.6 g, Protein: 1.1 g

CHILI PARSNIP

STEP 1
Wash the parsnip carefully and cut it into the strips.

STEP 2
Combine the chili pepper and cayenne pepper together.

STEP 3
Add lemon zest and ground black pepper.

STEP 4
Chop the shallot.

STEP 5
Combine the granulated garlic and chopped shallot together.

STEP 6
Add kosher salt and chili pepper mixture.

STEP 7
Then chop the dill and add it to the mixture too.

STEP 8
Squeeze the lemon juice into the chili mixture.

STEP 9
Sprinkle the parsnip strips with the chili mass and stir it carefully.

STEP 10
Then place the parsnip strips in the instant pot, add vegetable broth and close the lid.

STEP 11
Adjust the instant pot for 20 minutes and cook the dish.

STEP 12
When the time is over – transfer the cooked meal at the serving plates.

STEP 13
Enjoy!

 Cooking Difficulty: 2/10	 Cooking Time: 25 minutes	 Servings: 8

INGREDIENTS

- 15 oz. parsnip
- 1 tbsp. chili pepper
- 1 tsp. cayenne pepper
- 2 tbsps. olive oil
- ½ lemon
- 1 tbsp. lemon zest
- ½ c. fresh dill
- 1 tsp. ground black pepper
- 1 tsp. granulated garlic
- 1 tsp. kosher salt
- 3 oz. shallot
- 1 c. vegetable broth

NUTRITIONAL INFORMATION

Calories 83, Fat 3.7g, Carbs 12.22g, Protein 2g

DARK CHOCOLATE BARS

 Cooking Difficulty: 2/10

 Cooking Time: 5 minutes

 Servings: 12

INGREDIENTS
- 1 c. cocoa powder, unsweetened
- 3 tbsps. cacao nibs
- 1/8 tsp. sea salt
- 2 tbsps. maple syrup
- 1 ¼ c. chopped cocoa butter
- ½ tsps. vanilla extract, unsweetened
- 2 tbsps. coconut oil

STEP 1
Take a heatproof bowl, add butter, oil, stir, and microwave for 90 to 120 seconds until melts, stirring every 30 seconds.

STEP 2
Sift cocoa powder over melted butter mixture, whisk well until combined, and then stir in maple syrup, vanilla, and salt until mixed.

STEP 3
Distribute the mixture evenly between twelve mini cupcake liners, top with cacao nibs, and freeze for 1 hour until set.

STEP 4
Serve straight away.

NUTRITIONAL INFORMATION
Calories: 100, Fat: 9 g, Carbs: 8 g, Protein: 2 g

ALMOND MILLET CHEWS

INGREDIENTS

- 1 c. millet
- ½ c. almond butter
- ¼ c. raisins
- ¼ c. brown rice syrup

NUTRITIONAL INFORMATION
Calories: 100, Carbs: 15g, Fats: 5g, Proteins: 2g

 Cooking Difficulty: 2/10	 Cooking Time: 5 minutes	 Servings: 10

STEP 1

Melting the almond butter in the microwave for about twenty seconds. When this step is complete, place it into a mixing bowl with the brown rice syrup, raisins, and millets.

STEP 2

Once everything is blended well, use your hands to roll balls and place onto a plate. If desired, add a touch of more syrup to keep everything together. Place into the fridge for twenty minutes and then enjoy your dessert.

CHOCOLATE PEANUT BUTTER ENERGY BITES

 Cooking Difficulty: 1/10

 Cooking Time: 4 minutes

 Servings: 4

INGREDIENTS

- ½ c. oats, old-fashioned
- 1/3 c. cocoa powder, unsweetened
- 1 c. dates, chopped
- ½ c. shredded coconut flakes, unsweetened
- ½ c. peanut butter

STEP 1
Place oats in a food processor along with dates and pulse for 1 minute until the paste starts to come together.

STEP 2
Then add remaining ingredients, and blend until incorporated and very thick mixture comes together.

STEP 3
Shape the mixture into balls, refrigerate for 1 hour until set and then serve.

NUTRITIONAL INFORMATION
Calories: 88.6, Fat: 5 g, Carbs: 10 g, Protein: 2.3 g

RASPBERRY COMPOTE

 Cooking Difficulty: 3/10	 Cooking Time: 27 minutes	 Servings: 4

INGREDIENTS

- 2 c. raspberries
- 1 c. swerve
- 1 tsp. grated orange zest
- 1 tsp. vanilla extract

NUTRITIONAL INFORMATION

Calories 48, Fat 0.5g, Carbs 5g, Protein 1g

STEP 1
Plug in your instant pot and press the 'Saute' button. Add raspberries, swerve, orange zest, and vanilla extract. Stir well and pour in 1 cup of water. Cook for 5 minutes, stirring constantly.

STEP 2
Now pour in 2 more cups of water and press the 'Cancel' button. Seal the lid and set the steam release handle to the 'Sealing' position. Press the 'Manual' button and set the timer for 15 minutes on low pressure.

STEP 3
When you hear the cooker's end signal, press the 'Cancel' button and release the pressure naturally for 10-15 minutes. Move the pressure handle to the 'Venting' position to release any remaining pressure and open the lid.

STEP 4
Optionally, stir some more lemon juice and transfer to serving bowls.

STEP 5
Chill to a room temperature and refrigerate for one hour before serving.

SIMPLE BANANA COOKIES

 Cooking Difficulty: 2/10

 Cooking Time: 16 minutes

 Servings: 4

INGREDIENTS

- 3 tbsps. peanut butter
- 3 bananas
- ¼ c. walnuts
- 1 c. rolled oats

STEP 1
For a simple but delicious cookie, start by prepping the oven to 350. As the oven warms up, take out your mixing bowl and first mash the bananas before adding in the oats.

STEP 2
When you have folded the oats in, add in the walnuts and peanut butter before using your hands to layout small balls onto a baking sheet. Once this is set, pop the dish into the oven for fifteen minutes and bake your cookies.

STEP 3
By the end of fifteen minutes, remove the dish from the oven and allow them to cool for five minutes before enjoying.

NUTRITIONAL INFORMATION
Calories: 250, Carbs: 30g, Fats: 10g, Proteins: 5g

PEACH CRISP

 Cooking Difficulty: 2/10

 Cooking Time: 16 minutes

 Servings: 2

INGREDIENTS

- 2 tbsps. rolled oats
- 2 tbsps. brown sugar
- 2 diced peaches
- 1 tsp. sugar
- 3 tsps. coconut oil
- 4 tsps. flour

STEP 1
This recipe is built for two! You can begin by prepping the oven to 375 and getting out two small baking dishes.

STEP 2
As the oven begins to warm, take one of the mixing bowls and toss the peach pieces with the sugar, cinnamon, and a teaspoon of flour. When this is set, pour the peaches into a baking dish.

STEP 3
In the other bowl, mix together the three teaspoons of flour with the oats and the sugar. Once these are blended, pour in coconut oil and continue mixing. Now that you have your crumble place it over the peaches in the baking dish.

STEP 4
Finally, pop the dish into the oven for fifteen minutes or until the top is a nice golden color. If it looks finished, remove and cool before slicing your dessert up.

NUTRITIONAL INFORMATION
Calories: 110, Carbs: 20g, Fats: 5g, Proteins: 2g

COOKIE DOUGH BITES

 Cooking Difficulty: 1/10	 Cooking Time: 5 minutes	 Servings: 18

INGREDIENTS

- 15 oz. cooked chickpeas
- 1/3 c. vegan chocolate chips
- 1/3 c. and 2 tbsps. peanut butter
- 8 medjool dates pitted
- 1 tsp. vanilla extract, unsweetened
- 2 tbsps. maple syrup
- 1 ½ tbsps. almond milk, unsweetened

NUTRITIONAL INFORMATION
Calories: 200, Fat: 9 g, Carbs: 26 g, Protein: 1 g

STEP 1
Place chickpeas in a food processor along with dates, butter, and vanilla and then process for 2 minutes until smooth.

STEP 2
Add remaining ingredients, except for chocolate chips, and then pulse for 1 minute until blends and dough comes together.

STEP 3
Add chocolate chips, stir until just mixed, then shape the mixture into 18 balls and refrigerate for 4 hours until firm.

STEP 4
Serve straight away.

CONCLUSION

Possessing and using accurate information is vital if you want to make the most informed decisions in your life. Unfortunately, there is plenty of misleading information in the health and diet industry, and it can be confusing and frustrating. Don't go for the quick fix. Stick to the most sustainable, logical, healthy habits. It takes somewhere between 3 weeks and one month to create a habit. So, stick with it, and I am sure you will experience so many health benefits. It is my sincere hope that this book has been helpful to you. I hope that I have inspired you to bring yourself closer to the optimal levels of health you hope to obtain.

Considering all the ethical reasons for switching to a plant-based diet, the enormous health benefits and improved quality of life are the icings on an already extremely appealing cake.

Enjoy the journey!

Eva Evans

Printed in Great Britain
by Amazon

43448417R00129